ΛPPΛLΛCHIΛN
R E V I E W

VOL. 53, NO. 1
WINTER 2025

TRADITION. DIVERSITY. CHANGE.

ESTABLISHED IN 1973
PUBLISHED QUARTERLY
by Berea College
www.appalachianreview.net

©2025 by Berea College. Vol. 53, No. 1 Winter 2025. All rights reserved. No part of this publication may be reproduced without the prior permission of *Appalachian Review*. Periodicals postage paid at Berea, Kentucky, and at additional mailing offices. ISSN# 2692-9244 (Print); ISSN# 2692-9287 (Digital).

Electronic submissions only at www.appalachianreview.net. Distributed through a partnership between the University of North Carolina Press and Duke University Press. Basic subscription price: $32/year for individuals, $64/year for institutions. For subscription requests and inquiries, visit the magazine's website, email subscriptions@dukeupress.edu, or call 888-651-0122 (toll-free in the US and Canada) or 919-688-5134.

CONTENTS

EDITOR'S NOTE...................................*Jason Kyle Howard*   5

FICTION
Chelyen Davis
   Firewoman..   8
Heather Swain
   Bullfrog..   67

CREATIVE NONFICTION
Laura Johnsrude
   The Tiger in the Bin...   32
Makayla Danielle Gay
   The Call is Coming from Inside the House........................   99

POETRY
Heather Truett
   Legend...   22
   Ode to the Sky   24
   Bumble   26
   My Own Mythology..   28
   You almost cry, don't. You write..................................   30
John Schneider
   Portrait of an Empty House......................................   44
   Ragged Emerald..   47
Austin Sanchez-Moran
   Back East   48

Mac Collins
    Gregor, In Public 49
    Saturday Night 50
    Four Stanzas About 51
    Lawn ornaments 52
    Crossing the Apps 53
Luke Harvey
    Pulling In 65
    A-to-B 66
Evan Gurney
    Waiting Room 89
    Contrapasso for the Brain Damaged 90
Mikey Jones
    The Rainbow Trout 92
    Breathe 94
Daisy Bassen
    American Sonnet in the Time of a War, Not Our Own ... 97
Carrie Conners
    WV Muscle Memory 98
Erin Matheson Ritchie
    After the Fire 106
    Saratoga 107

INTERVIEW
George Singleton
    Wes Browne 54

CONTRIBUTORS 108

COVER PHOTOGRAPH
"Cincinnati" by Sean Foster

EDITOR'S NOTE

JASON KYLE HOWARD

February is the hardest month. Its brevity is deceptive. Those twenty-eight days stretch out, endless, seeming to drag and double in length. The promise of March—the promise of spring—is tantalizing, right there in front of us, the great tease. Even for someone who is fond of winter, as I am, it can seem endless.

Seasonal affective disorder (SAD) kicks into high gear. Stress at work, or at school, seems greater. For many, Valentine's Day brings feelings not of love but of loneliness. Or societal pressure. Even the many soups and stews that have sustained you throughout the season become bland and unexciting.

I'm reminded of Jane Kenyon's aptly titled poem "Depression in Winter," when the narrator recounts noticing "a little space between the south / side of a boulder / and the snow that fills the woods around it." She can take no more of the chill, the barren landscape, and finds herself sinking "with every step up to my knees…greedy for unhappiness."

And then: she finds a stone, surrounded by bare ground and "a patch of moss, bright green." Warmed by the sun, the rock becomes a source of hope. A promise.

As we muddle through the rest of the season—we're nearly there—my wish is that this issue of *Appalachian Review* can become that stone for you. A place of refuge where you can sense, where you can feel, the sun on your skin and the promise of good things to come.

These pages are filled with warmth. In the case of "Firewoman," a tour-de-force short story by Chelyen Davis, the heat is literal. Heather Swain's "Bullfrog," which finds a married mother of two at a moment of frustration and decision, will unsettle you. With its narrative of cleaning out her parents' home, Laura Johnsrude's essay "The Tiger in the Bin" takes the reader on a moving and relatable journey of memory. "The Call is Coming from Inside the House," a lyric essay by emerging writer Makayla Danielle Gay—whose debut poetry collection *Hackles* will be released in April—offers moving cultural and personal insights.

The poetry in this issue has been one of my stones this winter. I've felt the warmth of lines and words by Heather

Truett, John Schneider, Austin Sanchez-Moran and others. Beloved Southern writer George Singleton talks with Wes Browne, whose new novel *They All Fall the Same* is generating reader buzz and critical praise.

As you read, remember spring is in sight. Like the stone, I hope this issue will become your "secret porch of heat and light"—a refuge where, after you spend time, you can turn "back down" your path, "chastened and calm." ■

FIREWOMAN

CHELYEN DAVIS

The old house wanted to burn. It was fully on fire when the Markee Volunteer Fire Department's only truck, driven by Eb Peters, pulled up on the road in front of it. The truck was twenty-years-old, and we could use a new one, but we couldn't afford it. The Markee city budget no longer runs to new fire trucks—it doesn't even run to a paid fire department. We're all volunteers except

Timbo, the chief. The city pays for training, though, and your equipment. And your life insurance.

I got the call out in time to meet Eb at the station, so I rode in the truck, sirens blaring. In minutes we turned onto the Rock Creek Road, which leads out of town, and pulled up at the house, behind a line of beat-up pickup trucks with men hopping around, putting on their gear.

The house sat behind a narrow strip of front yard, and behind it a creek hugged against the foot of the hill. Cut into the hillside above was the train track, still in use, although the coal trains are fewer now, and it's been years since any miners washed the dust off their face in the house. The porch stretched the length of the house, and I imagined women sitting there, breaking beans, children running in the dirt yard, men leaned back in two-legged chairs.

But not for a long time. The dry old house burned gleefully.

It resisted every stream of water we threw at it, beams popping and cackling in defiance. As we sweated in our fireproof suits and aimed our hoses at its corners, it just kept burning. We beat back a flame in one place and it danced out in another. Beautiful reds and oranges leapt against the night sky.

The whole business was loud, like the house was shouting. The crack of the wood, the thrum of the flames, the hiss of the water. It was dramatic, celebratory, a little crazed. It reminded me of a Pentecostal service.

Finally the roof collapsed in an operatic whoosh, the house taking its final bow.

Timbo pulled off his helmet and told the crew to make sure it didn't get away from us and set the woods on fire. Then we'd have a real problem.

Truthfully, we hadn't tried too hard to put it out. We all knew the house was abandoned, given over to the mice and mud daubers' nests years ago. There was no one to rescue, nothing to save. It was a peeling, slanting eyesore.

That's why I'd set it on fire to start with.

Well, one of the reasons. But it's the one I like to focus on, where I'm doing Markee a favor. I don't do it too often. Just enough to trim the ragged edges off the town, spruce things up.

When the embers stopped pulsing and we'd soaked the smoking timbers and all the yard around it, Timbo declared us done. Eb and I took the truck back to the station. Timbo beat us there and was shucking off his suit when we hopped out of the truck. We pulled beers out of the minifridge and settled into the lawn chairs out front.

Timbo leaned his chair back against the station wall.

"I think that fire was funny," he said.

I took a sip of my beer. "Did it tell you a joke we couldn't hear?"

"Nobody likes a smartass, Dulcie," he said. "Funny suspicious, I mean."

"Like how?"

Timbo set his beer down so he could talk with his hands. He held them up, fingers wide, and I knew he was picturing the burning house. I pictured it too.

"Did you watch how it was burning? It wasn't just coming from one source. It looked like it had caught fire in different places at once."

"I didn't see that," I said. "Too busy aiming a hose at it."

"I'm going to go back in there tomorrow and have a look," Timbo said. "Too many fires around here for them all to be natural."

"What else would they be?" I said, hoping I didn't sound defensive. "No one even has insurance on these old places, so no one's trying to collect. There's just no point to it."

"That's what worries me," Timbo said, and threw his beer bottle at the trash can, hitting it perfectly.

■ ■ ■

Like I said, the house wanted to burn. They always do. They're done. Once they were full of working men and shouting children and worn-out women. Even if everyone was poor and everyone was tired, Markee had hummed.

I wasn't alive for its heyday, but I've heard stories. At one time, Markee had five bars, two movie theaters, and you could barely move on the streets on a Saturday, for all the holler folks come to town for the day.

When I was young, two of the bars and one of the theaters were still open. Now one bar is a diner, serving a passable breakfast and lunch, and the other gets the law called in every weekend to bust up fights.

And on streets all over town, some of the houses have been torn down—or burned, yes, and not all by me—and the street is like a set of broken teeth.

I figure, that's just the way it goes. I grew up on coal, but coal's dead. We all know it. Folks like to plaster black vinyl "Coal Keeps the Lights On" stickers across the backs of their trucks, but if some wind turbine company was to come offer them jobs with good pay and benefits, they'd be out in the yard with a paint scraper to get that vinyl off. Maybe they could stop holding their breath for the next downturn.

That's the ones that stayed, anyway. I can count up the high school classmates who left and didn't come back. I left too, for college, for a while. The guidance counselor helped me apply, told me that with an education, I could go anywhere I wanted. Charleston, even.

But I didn't like it out there. I didn't even leave West Virginia but nothing felt the same. The seasons didn't sit right on the land. Nothing felt familiar, and I didn't know it like I did Markee. It's not that I don't care to see the world. I just don't like to stay out there too long. Plus Dad had his heart attack, and I don't trust him to do his exercise, so I came on home.

I work at the diner, the one I said does a decent breakfast. A gravel-voiced chain smoker named Lucille has been the breakfast waitress there since before I was born, and I come in right after and see us through the lunch rush, such as it is.

I live with Dad, who's retired from hauling coal and mostly raises his garden and watches sports on TV, when he's not at

I smelled the smoke and watched those orange flames dance around and for the first time in a long time I didn't know what would happen next.

the diner with his buddies telling lies. They're done running their mouths by the time I come in. His gang goes in for artery-clogging breakfast platters. I tell him that's how he got the heart attack in the first place. He tells me he takes the walk his doctor said to do every day. I guess we'll see.

Anyway, it leaves me plenty of time to fight fires.

I didn't really join the Markee Volunteer Fire Department on purpose. Eb and Timbo were having lunch at the diner one day and saying how they were short on crew members because Gene Hawkins had died, of a heart attack in his own bed, which is how we'd all like to go. Something just grabbed me, and I heard myself say, "What do you have to do to be in the fire department?"

Eb probed a back molar with a toothpick and Timbo looked at me and said, "Well, you can come ride along and try it out next time we have a fire. Just don't get in the way."

"Ok," I said. "And that's it?"

Timbo picked up the check off the table, looked at the total, and pulled out his wallet.

"If you like it, we'll talk about training."

So that's what I did. I shadowed Eb and he put me in a fire suit, and I rode with him to the fire—a kitchen fire, somebody had put a Hungry Man in the oven and then got into watching the race on TV and forgot it. I smelled the smoke and watched those orange flames dance around and for the first time in a long time I didn't know what would happen next. We put it out pretty fast, but it could have gone another way. It was just about the best thing I'd done in I don't know how long. I told Timbo to train me on whatever I needed to know, that I wanted to be a fireman. Or a firewoman. And I've never been sorry.

■ ■ ■

Learning how to fight fires didn't directly tell me how to set them.

But it's not hard to work backward and connect the dots. I learned how to watch the flames move. I learned what kind of material burns fastest and hottest, and what burns slow. I learned a little bit about accelerants.

And I learned the Markee fire department—Eb and Timbo, and the others. I already knew Markee itself—which houses were abandoned, what hours people were out on the roads, what would look suspicious and what wouldn't.

I wouldn't say I've set a lot of fires. A shed on the Miller Creek road outside town was the first, just for practice. Then a falling-down house on Curtis Lane, then one on French Road. A shack on River Road, and now this one. That was over three years. I'm not crazy. They were all abandoned. Empty lots are better to look at.

How could I tell you what it's like? All the control and none of it at the same time. My choice of building, my plan, my match. Then the house takes over, runs the show, and anything could happen. We never got called out to the shed, it burned itself out. On French Road the sparks jumped to a tree behind the house, and we had to scramble to stop it from racing up the hillside. You just don't know what's going to happen. Unlike everything else.

Most days I know I'm going into the diner from ten till three. I'll go home, where Dad will be in his recliner, or in his garden. Every day follows the same track like a mule in harness, patiently trudging up and down the rows.

Fire doesn't do that. Fire jumps the track.

■ ■ ■

We had a weekly training session—that's what Timbo calls it, but mostly we just check the hoses and shine the truck. A couple of guys showed up that hadn't been there Saturday, so we retold it for their benefit.

"Somebody drove by and called it in, already fully engaged," Timbo said. "Burned fast, didn't it Dulcie?"

"Like a candle," I said. "It was determined to burn, no matter how much water we sprayed."

"You go back and look at it, Timbo?" said Eb. My stomach tightened.

"Yeah," Timbo said. "Some funny things about that fire. Burned too fast, burning from different spots on the house.

Went back out there yesterday. I'd say it'd be hard to prove if it was set on purpose or not. But I think it was."

"What would someone set it on fire for?" said Carl, who'd only been with the fire department a year, and had missed Saturday night because he had a job interview in Ohio.

"Dunno," Timbo said. "No trace of meth in there, so I don't think anyone was cooking in the house. No gas line. The power lines weren't live. I don't see how it could have set off accidentally. So if it wasn't an accident, why would someone want to burn it on purpose?"

"I had an aunt burned down her house for the insurance," Carl said. "Well, that's what I heard. They couldn't prove it, so she got the money. Built it back with a pool in it."

"Insurance fires I can understand," Timbo said. "Somebody benefits. Any time you got a crime, you got to look at who benefits. The motivation."

Timbo watches too many cop shows on TV.

"But who benefits from burning down an empty, falling-down house?" I asked, feeling like I'd been too quiet.

"Someone who likes it," Timbo said. "That's what worries me."

Carl said he'd let us know what he heard from the job in Ohio, but I knew if he got it he'd be gone. He'd meet a girl there, settle down, and he'd only come back for a weekend every now and then, although he would always call it coming home. I'm glad I don't have such a divided heart for where home is.

■ ■ ■

Timbo wasn't wrong. I did like it.

But I knew I'd been careful. I had waited for early evening, just enough light left to see my way inside. I'd packed my whole burning kit into a bag—rags, a lighter, some wicker and foam, a little can of kerosene. The ashes of an old rag could easily be found in an abandoned house. The kerosene would burn off, but if not, maybe somebody had just left some old kerosene in there. The wicker and foam, my accelerants, would burn fast. You can't prove there wasn't an old chair in there. All my evidence would burn.

I like to light the fire inside. I like to go in, connect with the place, let it know I'm setting it free. In the Rock Creek house, old wallpaper still hung, peeling, on the walls. The floors were cracked linoleum, and the carpeting that was so old you couldn't tell if it had a pattern, or even a color. A single curtain fluttered in a broken window. It could have felt like a horror story, but even in the gloom, it just felt sad. I set two little fires, one in the living room near the stairs, and one in the kitchen. And then I went home to wait for the call. You know the rest.

Timbo had said he didn't see anything he could prove. I hoped it stayed that way.

■ ■ ■

I kept my head down for a while. On Thursdays we trained, and Timbo didn't bring up his worries. Summer brought us brush fires, so it was something to do, although a brush fire isn't anything like a house fire. There's nothing interesting about a brush fire—just figuring out where it's going and trying to stop it from getting there. We had a fire in a garage, where a spark hit some solvent, and we got called out to a couple of car accidents. All routine.

I just worked and helped Dad in his garden. He always planted too much, but I didn't want to say plant less. It seemed like a concession to age—if he planted less, I was afraid that next thing he'd do less, and then he'd just sit in that recliner and wait to die. I'd seen enough men wither like that, going from hale and hearty to shuffling behind a walker once they stopped moving. The only way to outrun age, I figured, was to not slow down enough for it to catch up.

But he did tire more easily since the heart attack. At night I washed the dishes, while Dad fell asleep in his recliner, TV blaring. I sat out on the porch in the dark, clammy night, and wondered when it would be safe to think about my next fire.

■ ■ ■

"I found it," Timbo said the next Thursday, after we'd watched a training video on putting out fires with foam. "Knew if I looked hard enough, I'd find it."

"Find what?" said Carl, who was moving to Ohio that weekend.

"Proof," Timbo said. "Proof that Rock Creek fire was set."

I felt like the bottom was gone from my stomach.

"It was a flash burn," Timbo said. "Found a scorch pattern in two places. Stairwell and kitchen, or thereabouts."

"What are you going to do?" Carl asked.

"Not sure," Timbo said. "Gotta think on that one."

■ ■ ■

It was coming on spring. We'd weathered the cold winter, me and Dad and his TV, and finally it was time to think about planting, just as much as last year. Time to go outside and see what the winter had done. Time to prune things back so they could grow again.

I'd had my eye on the old store for awhile. Two stories, wooden, paint peeling off the RC Cola logo on its side. It had been a general store, then a feed store, then a thrift store slash Christian bookstore, before it finally wasn't anything at all. The apartment above hadn't had a renter in ten years. It wasn't on the way to anywhere. Time had moved on and left it sitting there. Waiting for me.

I picked an afternoon in late March, double-checked my supplies, and slipped in through the back, away from the street.

Inside, a few old bookshelves stood at crazy angles. The ceiling was pressed tin, rusting. Dust motes floated in a late beam of sunlight. I checked upstairs, just so I'd know

I'd had my eye on the old store for awhile. Two stories, wooden, paint peeling off the RC Cola logo on its side.

no living thing was up there, not even a bird. All I saw was a soulless place, cheaply renovated, peeling Formica and cracked plaster.

I laid my fires and backed out of the house, satisfied. I was already thinking about how it would look an hour from now from behind the firehose, when I heard a footstep behind me.

"I don't know if I'm surprised or not," Timbo said.

The shock jolted a scream out of me.

"Back in," Timbo said, spinning his finger in a circle. "Let's put out your fires, and then we'll talk."

He pulled a fire extinguisher from a backpack and drowned my fledgling fires. Then he turned a bookcase over on its side and sat down on one end, gesturing me to the other.

"How'd you know?" I asked.

"Know it was you, or know where to find you?"

"Both."

"I got to thinking about that fire. And the one before that, on River Road. The one on French Road. The one up in the Clarke subdivision."

"That one wasn't me."

He raised an eyebrow.

"Well. We've had more fires since you joined the fire department. That's the first thing I thought about. And then I thought about why. When nobody benefits, what's the motive? Someone's getting something out of setting that fire. And I figured, if they're not getting money, and they're not getting revenge on somebody, then they're getting kicks out of it. They enjoy it. And that means they either enjoy watching it burn, or they enjoy fighting it. Setting themselves a challenge."

He scuffed at the dust on the floor with the toe of his work boot.

"You're a smart girl, Dulcie. I know you want to be like all the other guys in the department, and you hang out and drink beer and everybody's buddies. But you're not like the other guys. You're smarter. You don't have to be here working at the diner. And that's your choice, I know how it is. But I've known people like you, who need a challenge. I figure you joined the fire department because you were bored. And I can see when we're out at fires, you're not bored. You're into it. So I put two and two together. I know everybody in this town, and I only know one person bored enough to set buildings on fire."

He looked at me, like it was my turn. My turn to tell him he was right, or make excuses, or explain that yes, it was that, but it was other things too. I was restless in this town, and I loved this town, and it was all tied up together.

I couldn't explain all that. So I asked the easier question.

"How'd you know I'd be here?"

"Followed you."

Maybe I should watch more of Timbo's cop shows. I couldn't even spot a tail in a town of 600.

"What are you gonna do?"

Timbo sighed.

"You know, I went to college too. I ever tell you that? No? Well, I did. Three years, anyway. Studied forestry. Then my dad died. No more college money, no more money period unless Mom or I one got a job. Plus there was Charla, you know, still in high school."

Timbo and his sister Charla were both years older than me, and I only knew her as a character in his stories and a minivan with North Carolina tags that appeared on holidays and for a week in the summer. Timbo took off work to go fishing with nephews whose whole idea of what it meant to be mountain boys was what Timbo taught them. I imagined them swaggering back to their flatland schools with tales of trout and bears and copperheads, mountain caves and haints and grapevine swings. That's the sort of thing he'd show them, in a week. You'd have to stay longer to know more.

"But you stayed," I said. "Even after Charla was gone."

"Time passed," he said. "Pretty soon it felt too late to go back. Plus I'd settled in. I'm like you in a way. Comfortable and restless here, both. I just finally decided on comfortable. Markee's my home, and I reckon I'll stay put. Besides, these old coal towns, they start losing people, then they lose services, and before you know it, they're not even towns, they're just houses that happen to sit in a row. I don't want that for Markee."

"I don't either," I said.

"What do you want, then?"

I didn't know what I wanted. Excitement. Challenge. To cut off the dying parts of the town and hope it saved the good parts. When I'd been out in the world, I'd been homesick for the place I now rubbed up against, trying to smooth it and me down so we could fit together.

"I reckon I want to stay," I said.

"Then you've got to quit burning shit down," Timbo said. "Arson's a felony, you know. I ought to turn you in."

A felony seemed unfair. "But nobody was hurt," I said. "I was careful."

"But it's wrong," Timbo said. "It's not healthy for you either. What would you do if you were me?"

The question hung in the gloom, and I didn't know what to tell him. Nothing he could do would fix a thing. He couldn't cure me being bored or Markee fading away. What would punishment serve? I'd just be bored in prison.

"I'll stop," I said. "I promise. No more fires."

"I wonder," Timbo said. "I wonder if you can stick to it. I wonder if you can be a firefighter and squash the arsonist in you."

"I can," I said, not sure at all.

"It's getting dark, we better get on out of here while we can see our feet," he said.

He checked my fires to make sure they were out. We went out the back, same as we'd come in.

In the street, he turned to me. "My advice to you, Dulcie, is get comfortable, or get gone. That's not a threat. But I care about this town too, and I can't let you burn it down. And you can't live torn up like this. You want to stay? Good. I hope it sticks. Make up your mind to be satisfied or move on."

He walked down the street toward his truck. And I started the walk home, as the sunset died over the hills above town. ■

LEGEND

Reimagined Voice for the Biblical Jael

I awake old, new wrinkles on my hands, dark spotted
weapons no one else can wield. They are the only
parts of me that feel as if they belong to me, to the woman
who became a story, a god-tool, the slayer

of one soldier. I am that story, told and untold,
crafted to fit a judge's need, whispered, held beneath
tongues to melt any sign of disobedience, painted onto the skin
of a child's discipline, a husband's rage. I lived to become a warning.

So long since I have raged.

In secret, I unmake mothers, unmake mistakes, unmake
the beds of another time and place. Veiled faces do not rise
to meet my eyes unless the moon is high in the sky and the men
are gone. I am a woman for other women, alone.

My tent is nearly empty in this desert, holding only
what I make for my own use. I do not go to the marketplace. I feed
my body with what everyone thinks they know, so much, eating legends
for breakfast and lunch, dining on deeds that no one will ever forgive.

They don't even pretend to forget.

The only sound for miles, the music of chimes I crafted, these
aging hands heating and hammering, knuckles and wrists
wrenched, molten heat in one thin line, until each shining
metal peg, each day between then and now, rang and sang its melody.

Another moon is coming, a new cycle spins. My goat is tied
to a stake. The milk is fresh and cool. I am alone in the noon
sun, and the past is a thick drink of this new harvest. The cream
of a saint's violence has risen to the top.

My hammer only sings for me.

ODE TO THE SKY

You ignored the ground before I lived, skipped out of the fox
whole, held to earth's satisfied hands. You are fake

leaving, large like the mile of mouth straightening away
from the tip of a narrow knife. Prism filled, not comforting,

a silencing, a singularity that stops with eyes closed or giving
up against a grassland, a corpse walking away or blowing away

my voice, clear and warrior strong. I am released from our space
in a gown, spewing silk over wasted breast, parting my next

eternity. I won't be cold. My boxspring is a pond, fertile,
ocean-full. A flight away from staying, your light caressing

empty, folding up the sun. My freedom not exposed, a danger
place with pomegranate dirt. Breathe air detached from skin, a naked

modern man, despairing death, a lie. You stop acting as if creation is constructed and now un-made. I don't have a softness.

It is me sinking like the round moon, your barrenness, my fish. It is me free under the stream, you spitting moths and toad frogs. It is not me

crying against you in this absence… already my living is no one. You can pluck the nowhere from my chaos. You did bury that little gem of joy.

There is not a solid hue stopped in that wilting dark prism of a forest. I splash into the algae's glow   alone.

HEATHER TRUETT

BUMBLE

I don't want to be a honeybee. I just want to bumble
bee my way through, queen
of a messy hive with not a single
hexagonal sweet inside. I will be bigger. I will have
more hair to tangle
your fingers in. I will paint
my body pollenate
and share my food
with you. I will nourish
us, keep our community
small, our love buzz tender
in the grass.

The honeybee nurtures the world, offers herself
in tea and pastry, sweet and sacrificial, dying
from one sting, but not me. I wield
a sword, a dagger,
a knife, all my life, pry

free the pain of protecting
self, learning hard ways
again and again, sharp
stinger for survival,
sewing blades of grass

with my needle end. I don't need
the heavy hive to make our home. I am
queen without the sticky crown, burrow
down in dirt with me. Let's be
alone this summer day. Let's live
and die to our own bodies vibrating
beneath a green sea of grass.

HEATHER TRUETT

MY OWN MYTHOLOGY

after Ama Codjoe

1. It was a bright white mall and we were in another country, my husband and I and a large group of teens. I kissed a woman whose skin smelled of honey.

2. I was in Honduras. It was summer. We took the kids to the mall for dinner and ice cream. A woman kissed me outside the food court.

3. I was sitting in a chair beside Baskin Robbins. There was a woman talking on her phone. She met my eyes. She kissed me.

4. It was a case of mistaken identity, the summer I sat on a bench in a mall and was kissed by a woman who thought I was somebody else.

5. No, she didn't think I was somebody else. She thought I was me, and we were lovers in a past life, and at last we were reunited. With a kiss.

6. We were never lovers. I do not know her name. She spoke rapid Spanish into a cell phone, paused beside my chair, and then she kissed me.

7. Someone somewhere, the person on the phone, dared this woman with the wild curls to kiss the next stranger she saw, and that was me.

8. No one dared anyone to do anything. My lips still tasted of sugar and milk. Something about me called to her across the crowd.

9. We were in an ancient land, where I did not belong, but my lips did, and her lips did, meet in the middle of the white stone halls.

10. I was in a mall in Honduras. I spoke very little Spanish. It was June. Or July. She wore a dress that flowed around her like wine when she kissed me.

11. My favorite Honduran poet once kissed me in a mall in Tegus, her ink-dipped lips leaving lyrics behind in my mouth.

12. The woman who kissed me in the mall in Honduras was not the poet I love so much. She was no one I had ever met before.

13. It was the summer of strawberry ice cream, our mouths met, lips with no lengua, no necesitamos las palabras en el verano de helado de fresa.

HEATHER TRUETT

YOU ALMOST CRY, DON'T. YOU WRITE

his hands and scalpel images from page
and line, but your insides are lined
with dopamine hits, and you aren't sure grief counts

when ache is tied to taut balloon strings, helium
huffed into the sky. You ink his words
onto inner arm and ink his heart onto

computer screens, but where is his heart?
The University of South Carolina Medical School.
You write coldly of it not pumping. It is lying,

its cage of ribs in a freezer. You write like ice,
grieve like memory's a box, a lock,
just the tip above the water, the finger

tips along the spine of a body
almost no one touched, a body literally
out of air, twin balloons too heavy

to float. He sank, and you are sinking
into the future, letting the days river
over chemicals that stop the other chemicals

from gutting you, like they're gutting him
on the silver slab of an education. You graduate
this December, while he holds

his pride in you against the tide of glaciers bearing
down feathers and unrecognizable grief. You
almost cry. Then don't.

THE TIGER
IN THE BIN

LAURA JOHNSRUDE

I am the caretaker of a permanent
collection, a museum of qualified
superlatives. Pieces have accrued over
a long time and need collating and tagging,
yes, but the whole exhibition reveals the
flavor of our family—the theme, minus
the things we regret tossing out, minus
items eaten or worn out or loaned to other
institutions.

As manager of the store, I'm fascinated by an Icelandic practice described by A. Kendra Greene in her book, *The Museum of Whales You Will Never See*. Greene noticed commonplace objects in home window dioramas, set facing whoever is outside looking in.

In our dining room window, I imagine setting out my son Ben's matchbox cars—in a train, as he used to do—and settling my daughter Sarah's handmade earrings and pottery among the toys. At one edge of the window, I could prop up my grandfather's poetry journal inscribed to him from my grandmother: *to J.F.J. from M.V.O.* At the other end, I'd pose the jeans jacket Sarah wore for a decade and the purple slip-on shoes Ben wore in elementary school.

Each month, I could lower the blinds and create the next scene. Keeping it fresh for the audience.

■ ■ ■

Breast cancer stifled something in me, five years ago. A vague sense of nihilism came over me, amplified, more recently, by the pandemic years. I may never buy another lamp, another clock, another bedside table. We have enough, I declared. Time to start pushing things out the door.

It's not so easy, though.

I'm particularly paralyzed by the stuff Sarah and Ben left behind, not completely sure what is theirs, what is mine. The kids don't live here anymore, but the upstairs jack-n-jill bedrooms are still full of their things. Adults, now, they've moved to other states—north and west—and settled onto sofas dragged from sidewalks, thumped up concrete steps, over thresholds, into small spaces without televisions or landline phones. When one of them visits, I am careful in my timing, suggesting, offhandedly, "Maybe later you could look through the stuff in your bureau?" But they are busy/disinterested/overwhelmed/anxious and "maybe later" rarely comes. I'm generally alone on a floor, mulling over what each piece means, why I shouldn't drop it into the trash, or the recycling, or the donation pile.

Not long ago, Ben and I were in our basement storage room looking for a good mailer box. My back was to him as I sifted through various sizes of cardboard containers. When I stood up and turned around, I saw my grown son lift one corner of a plastic bin and slip his hand inside to touch the head of his childhood companion, the Calvin and Hobbes stuffed tiger he'd slept with and carried in his backpack on airport trips. *Pat, Pat, Pat.* Then he withdrew his hand and popped closed the corner.

So, Hobbes is safe, then, having cleared the bar of essential worth.

When no one is left who remembers the medals and costumes, they will be easy to toss.

When no one remembers, they will be trash.

■ ■ ■

In my parents' garage, an old mattress stood on end along with a single-bed metal frame. Nearby, a light blue and white playpen was collapsed into a netted square.

"Daddy, why are you keeping that mattress?"

"Maybe Sarah or Ben will want it someday."

"But they don't live in North Carolina. They don't even live in Kentucky. Sarah bought her own mattress when she moved to New York."

Daddy shrugs.

"And the playpen?"

"I could probably give away the playpen."

That playpen looks like trash, to me. Wouldn't meet safety codes. Must be mildew in the fabric, rust in the hinges. But Daddy leaves it there, against the garage wall, as though someone will want it, that soft tent where children babbled and pulled to standing, reached out their arms to be picked up.

I unrolled brown grocery bags stored in front of where Daddy parks his Chevrolet. Inside one, I found old Simplicity and Butterick sewing patterns, and my thoughts flashed back to a fabric store somewhere in Winston-Salem, North Carolina, where I sat atop a high stool looking at oversized hardcover books, too heavy to lift. I turned shiny pages of tall, skinny ladies modeling the latest fashions, entertaining myself while Mom and Grandmother Jarratt chose fabrics for my new clothes. Wish I'd paid more attention so I could tell you what they said to one another, but I can only imagine them whispering about the cost and which materials were appropriate for a church dress. Maybe Mom felt inadequate since she couldn't sew, and she was beholden to her mother, who could. Maybe Grandmother Jarratt shifted aside the patterns with skirts too short, the fabrics with colors too loud.

I was required to take home economics in junior high, long ago, when the Watergate hearings were being televised. My efforts resulted in a blousy sleeveless top with the flowery collar sewn on upside down. It's saved in one of my own basement bins, collar now right-side up.

In the middle of the garage, Daddy opened a tall ladder and asked me to hand up the Christmas decorations. My eighty-two-year-old daddy climbed up the rungs to that point where I'd feel dizzy, then he told me to give him the Christmas tree shaped out of wood, spray-painted green. And then the blue box. And then the decorative rugs. And then the large flat rectangular box, the kind that would fit under a bed. Daddy sat each item on a square of plywood in the ceiling of the garage directly over where he parked his car. He'd figured out how to stack each item so the lot would fit in the space and not fall on our heads.

"You know, Daddy, if you got rid of some of the items around the edge of the garage, you wouldn't have to climb up here every year to store the Christmas decorations."

He cleared his throat and didn't answer for a few seconds. "I know that."

I drove to Target and bought clear plastic containers and sat outside with a rag and the brown grocery bags. One by one, I wiped dust and dead bugs off the sewing patterns,

Maybe they'd left all that stuff in the garage to decay into rust and ash, one item falling into the one below, like strata of sedimentary rock.

moving them from the risk of water and mold into a storage container made of materials not in existence when these things were first put in the attic, before landing in the garage.

My parents didn't ask me to put that stuff into plastic bins. They didn't even seem excited by what I'd found in the grocery bags. Maybe they'd left all that stuff in the garage to decay into rust and ash, one item falling into the one below, like strata of sedimentary rock. And here I came along and disrupted their plans.

■ ■ ■

Nana, my mother-in-law, moved into a retirement community four years ago and her big house stands empty of people most of the time. Her five kids keep discussing what to do with it, when to sell it. It's expensive to keep up an empty house. The insurance, the lawn, the electricity, the property taxes.

Then there's all the stuff.

My sister-in-law manages the finances and is the caretaker of Nana's collection. She suggested we inventory each item, room by room, and maybe, whenever one of us visits, we can do a room, or a closet. Type the details into an Excel document, shareable online. We all responded with silence.

We'll all be there soon, for Christmas—Nana's five children, and spouses of her children, and her eight grandchildren— filling up the spaces and walking past clocks and framed portraits, sitting on the sofas and chairs, rummaging through holiday storage boxes, smiling at one another.

On the second floor, there's one narrow closet filled completely with artwork, many created by Nana. She can't remember all the details, though, so we'll pull out pieces and stare at them.

"Is it one of hers?"

"I don't recognize it."

"The next one, behind it, the one with the abstract people and houses?"

"I don't know."

And the closet will feel small with the dim light and all those canvasses looming and leaning, and we'll feel uneasy, worried we will not know which paintings were created by our mother/mother-in-law/grandmother. We should be able to tell.

■ ■ ■

In an essay about "clutter," the author made a distinction between terminal materialism and instrumental materialism, connecting the former to things that will become obsolete, and the latter to things we value for their meaning, for their association to experiences and people in our memories. The adjective "instrumental," though, conjures objects valued for their usefulness—the best whisk, or vacuum cleaner, or stapler. Those items that stay in our homes—because they are our tools—until they are worn out. We may be disappointed when we drop them into the garbage or recycling bin, but we do not weep.

"Instrumental materialism" is inadequate to describe the stuff I wrap in tissue paper or settle back on bookshelves. The stuff that makes me sigh. The stuff of echoes, symbolizing the whos and whats of my already-happened life.

"Associative materialism" would be a better term. Or metaphorical materialism. Sensory materialism. Representative materialism. Flashback materialism. Fragile materialism.

Until-I-have-dementia materialism.

If I can remember my dad pulling the kids in the little red wagon, I am still here. If I can remember lying on a bean bag beside Ben's bed and reading aloud *My Side of the Mountain,* I am still here. If I can remember Sarah clutching her stuffed dog Patch to her cheek, her wispy baby hair around her face, I am still here. They are still here.

■ ■ ■

When Mom handed down my great-great-grandfather's Civil War-era Union soldier's trunk, years ago, I inherited the old books inside. Math and English textbooks. An oversized illustrated history book: *The Story of the Spanish-American War and the Revolt in the Philippines.* A guidebook for how young ladies should behave. Some volumes bear my aunt's name, or my maternal grandfather's name, written inside the front cover. They are long dead, but see, here are their books.

This summer, I lifted the books out, one by one, and spread them out on the carpet. Brittle, some pages loose. I asked my daughter, asked my son, asked my sister, asked my brother, "Do you want any of these?" I asked a local university librarian and a history professor and an artist, "Do you want any of these?"

No one wanted any of the books, but I can't put them in the trash because Aunt Hazel took me to see *Mary Poppins*, and she took me to visit Old Salem where I levered water out of an old pump on the town square, and Grandaddy Jarratt is standing beside toddler me, in an old photo, and he wrote poetry and had trouble finding a job.

So I push the plastic bin of books back against the concrete wall of an unfinished subterranean room, the one that leaks in a hard rain.

■ ■ ■

Waters rushed into homes in Eastern Kentucky, one recent July, drowning dolls and tablecloths and Christmas ornaments. Tornados blew apart homes in Western Kentucky, not long ago, scattering baseball hats and wedding dresses and baby clothes. An apocalypse of non-sorting, a devil-sent destruction of all the stuff, indiscriminately, both the loved and the unloved. Media outlets posted photos of wind-strewn objects over there, and floating baskets over here, private belongings weathering without roofs, without walls, without boxes. A woman in a doorway with her dog, standing in mud. A bearded man in a baseball hat sitting in the middle of a great pile of stuff—the corner of a bedframe, upturned cabinets, splayed shirts, rumpled pants, a green ball.

■ ■ ■

My mom used to object when I offered to go through their magazines to separate the "keepers" from the recycling pile. But she hardly notices when I do it, now.

I sit on the floor in the corner bedroom where I sleep during my visits—my brother's old room—and sift through old junk mail and the tall pile of magazines stored under the bureau there, peeling off address labels as I go. *Southern Living. Our State.* Baptist church periodicals. I do the same thing in my parent's bedroom, with a stack left in a large book bag. Wake Forest University bulletins. Blue Ridge Parkway magazines. In the den, I tackle the largest towers beneath the sofa side table and on the white brick hearth. *Time.* Country music glossies. *Good Housekeeping.*

I find a few of Mom's notes to herself—lists for her church library, reminders about upcoming appointments—and I set them aside to keep, scraps of when she knew what day it was and who was hosting book club. I pause and hold up greeting cards and church bulletins, asking Dad, "Save or toss?" I stumble over the old *Oxford American*s, as I have trouble recycling that literary magazine in my own home. All those unread essays, poems, and short stories paralyze me, so I organize them by date and return them to the shelf.

After I dump the last armful into Daddy's huge roller recycling bin, I hold my phone out and over the inside-the-trashcan view and take a photo of the pile, proud of my success. I'd culled hundreds of volumes from my parents' house, decluttered their environment. But I pause, there on the back patio. I don't send the photo to my sister, Amy, or post it to Instagram. I feel a bit ashamed of my hubris. Maybe I'd made a mistake, been presumptuous, sifting for trash in my childhood home, a house that I can no longer call my own.

I could have declared the middle bedroom—Amy's old room—to be the museum of magazines, indexed the lot, and arranged tasteful displays along the dresser top, the side tables, the shellacked trunk under the light switch. I could have hung pretty shelves and set potted plants between the

I feel a bit ashamed of my hubris. Maybe I'd made a mistake, been presumptuous, sifting for trash in my childhood home, a place that I can no longer call my own.

home décor magazines and the university bulletins. I could have designed labels with red and blue and green Garamond font and created an archive for our descendants.

At the bottom of the refuse bin, the magazines are rubbish.

Catalogued and curated, they would have been a mini-reference library of family periodicals.

■ ■ ■

I drag up a heavy wooden-framed standing easel from the basement and out onto my front porch where I slap at it, with a rag, brushing off spider webs and dust. Sarah said I could give it away. With a wet cloth, I wipe down the blackboard, on one side and, less effectively, the dry-erase board on the other side. As a kid, my artsy daughter had painted on paper clipped to the dry-erase face, so she left behind indelible swaths of primary colors. The easel was a sturdy piece of playroom equipment though. Would be handy for an after-school community center. I manhandled it into the garage and opened the garage door, ready to load it into my trunk. Sunshine fell on the thing and illuminated the vertical letters down the lower left-hand leg below the blackboard, drawn in turquoise paint.

I LOVE TO DO ART

Oh, Sarah. I'll have to keep it now.

■ ■ ■

Guy Clark invites us to notice the little things in a song he wrote a long time ago, and Lyle Lovett gave the tune life, many times over. "Step inside this house," Lyle sings, pointing out the picture on the wall "painted by a friend . . . it doesn't look like much I guess but it's all that's left of him." On he goes, sweetly, reverently, gesturing to his treasures—a poetry book, a gift from a girl; a piece of glass which casts a rainbow; a guitar from an old man; and his boots and vest and jacket and leather bag and his "hat hangin' on the wall." Ordinary things belonging to him. Which is the entire point, of course. Life is made of the ordinary stuff endowed with meaning. When Lyle sings the song, it hurts to listen.

■ ■ ■

In my parents' house, I found a heavy scrapbook Mom made, documenting my wedding preparations, thirty-five years ago. Her handwritten notes, both wry and sweet, in ink.

There's the receipt for the groom's wedding ring: $121.22.

There's my signature, forged by Mom, on the venue agreement.

I'd never seen the scrapbook before, never knew of its existence. But here it was, in my lap, in the den where I grew up, in the house my parents have owned since 1967. I gasped. "Mom, you did this?" But Mom doesn't know, can't remember anymore, and she looked, wide-eyed, back at me. "I did?" was what her face said.

I turned the pages and read bits aloud, conjuring new images of Mom bending over the oval dining room table, scissors in hand, trimming edges, collating her own experiences into a paper documentary of the months leading up to the wedding of her firstborn. My librarian Mom, careful to include the "will not attend" cards, thoughtful with her neat penmanship, preserving on paper what she will one day forget.

I think of some notepad pages found, earlier, amongst the junk mail, like a stray diary entry, intimate and fragile. Mom had written seven almost-identical sentences, like a mantra: "Now tonight I have somehow come to believe I will always remember tonight and what it means to me . . ." Minor differences between the lines, her plea to not forget, penned so carefully, like a prayer, ending with, "So as I leave this place where I now find myself, I do still believe I will always remember this night."

She'd known, then, what was coming, what was leaving.

Wedding scrapbook still open, I looked up at Mom and at Dad and at my sister, Amy.

"Can I have this?" I asked them, the people of the house.

"Is it mine?" I asked the room. ■

PORTRAIT OF AN EMPTY HOUSE

*Japan has more than 10 million vacant houses throughout
rural areas known as "akiya", Japanese for "empty or
abandoned house."*

This is where the ghosts live, in the joinery
holding paulownia chests, and in centuries-old

wooden floors crafted to absorb stories
that once rained through these rooms— now buckling—

in this long vacant Kyoto country house.
The kiri tree planted to honor the daughters birth,

has been harvested to assemble a bridal chest
of drawers: her dowry preserved with wooden dowels

and metal pulls, hinges and locks. Now what cannot
be possessed remains, only in memories

survived by dovetail mortise and tenon joints.
No longer postponed. No longer unspoken.

■ ■ ■

A cold wind chills the vacant house. Deserted.
Come morning, the windows fill with light—

the rooms remain dark. Children hurry on, grown, ripened
like persimmons dangling on the branch,

planted in the shadow of the kiri tree.
The black night sky shines like a river that freezes

come winter, waits for the heavens to open,
for the hard brightness of dreams to enter,

as feet scurry to find new daylight. The chest
grandpa toiled to put together

now a melody you could not sing—yet won't forget.

■ ■ ■

What tender songs of longing these ghosts
orchestrate, an evensong for swallows

arriving in the absence of light, to call this home.
Here past and present do meet, as remembrance,

like spirits of broken kin they linger—as if—
trying to find each other before the dark

returns, all that's left of a house in the waning
light that remains, circling, the wood rotting.

Having done its job, the sturdy post and beam structure
sags in ghosted air, mournful of the past.

While the swallows hold a lonely vigil,
their wings move like tiny arms grasping

for what was lost. Like regret, they come
and go out through our broken windows.

Ancestral doors—as by custom—
await the warmth of family

to fill our abandoned spaces with future life.

JOHN SCHNEIDER

RAGGED EMERALD

From 7000 feet atop this peak, I struggle
to keep to an ill-defined trail, rise above
finalities, sense some truth within

the distant glimmer of Tahoe's Emerald Bay,
still ethereal. Today, Fannette Island's outline
is uncertain, its irregular edges

almost the shape of tragedy, the branches
of its hundred year old Jeffrey pines no longer
brushing the heavens—no longer evergreen,

skeletal, no more dreams of resurrection.
Without farewell song, all bodies eventually
sink below a once pristine surface. Planted

like a stone marker alongside half-remembered
family histories and the vague warnings we add

to them, a dark spot on a well-lit x-ray:
imperfectly shaped, ragged as some impossible
island, emerald as only death can be,
the water soft, almost vulnerable as flesh,

almost inviting.

JOHN SCHNEIDER

BACK EAST

The foreboding of a twilit field of corn
when a thunderstorm cruises along
a prairie sky and you're in a crappy Saab
And you're supposed to be back East
but this is your home, and back East
is where thunderstorms get cut down
by the ocean or the city, that seems to pretend
to solve everyone's loneliness with more people
and there is definitely enough gas
to speed down a dark road,
and that flying, throbbing feeling can only
come from those last two miles before
the interstate hugs your hometown
and you are dropped off down the block
and you run down a leaf-speckled sidewalk
to the shadow of an unlocked white door
through to your bed that will always be empty
unless you come home to sleep in it.

AUSTIN SANCHEZ-MORAN

GREGOR, IN PUBLIC

The air smells lovely
this afternoon, now
that we are finished
with the casual firebombing
of the willows, rivers,
and crimson maples,
laying fresh coats of ash
and dust on concrete.
The sunset is no longer
split by the mountains
and the little old lady
who usually walks around
the block three times a day
must be on vacation
somewhere in the Maldives.
The house sparrow's
summary execution is scheduled
for right now
and that potato salad
expired yesterday.
Someone, up ahead,
is failing to use a musty
road flare to signal death
toward an oozing accident
and, like anyone else,
I scamper away from sudden
and bright lights, chittering
to myself about how
immediate this has all been.

MAC COLLINS

SATURDAY NIGHT

I ignored the moon
for you on the walk home.
It was dark, and the air
was light and warm.
A dry heat,
the sun in hiding.
Nothing that frozen
raspberries can't fix.
I ought to tear the fishnets
off your bag of tangerines
and feast for a moment
upon entering our home,
but I am tired tonight
and you are sleeping.
The snapdragons
in the crystal vase
have mostly wilted, not yet
skulls, fleshless and wincing.
They droop, flaccid enough
to trace gentle lines in sand,
swaying in the winds coming
through the open balcony.
I hope they are strong
enough for the weight
of a hummingbird
alighting on their slender stems.
Soon this vase will be empty,
but the market will come again.

MAC COLLINS

FOUR STANZAS ABOUT

The patch of dog chewed concrete
is ferociously barren
save for a few pieces of kibble
left over from trying to tame
a wild cat.

A bit of dust blows
from where a patch of grass
used to be
speckled with flowering clovers
and bumblebees.

I think I saw a cloud
last week,
patchy, wispy, sulking
in the sky.
A teenager's untrimmed beard.

Thankfully the rain pours
in the supermarket
making my forgetting
to water the pianos
in the garden a moot point.

MAC COLLINS

LAWN ORNAMENTS

Pink, pink, pink, pink, pink moon

Tonight the moon will be pink
from gorging on brine shrimp and
because I want it to be pink.
It'll be up there standing on one leg
(other tucked up close to torso),
preening broken feathers that flitter
and float on the surface of an isomalt
swamp in south-central Florida.
I want the mayflies to be missing
(perhaps too worn out from being whipped
around by old men in waders),
but leave the creamsicle dragonflies
dripping orange on cattails
and glinting alligator eyes. Hatchlings
will grunt for marshmallows tossed over
the side of an airboat. The little blue
heron will gaze up at the night sky
and wish it knew what kind of blush
a flamingo wears to get such deep shades
of pink and it will all be so beautiful
because I need it to be.

MAC COLLINS

CROSSING THE APPS

The rain drops rap
the mountain maple leaves
and salamanders lull
on soaked sponge moss.
Lightning licks the horizon
and a black bear blushes,
fooled again by honey-
suckle. Over the hills
is the rolling thunder
of thirty-seven
war elephants harrumphing
through the rainforest.
Hannibal, take
the turnpike. The toll
is cheap and bypasses
the twenty-two hundred mile
scenic route. I beg you leave
me be, loblolly and white
pines keep my winters
green enough and I have
already sowed my seeds
in this valley. Look,
the huckleberry
is taking root
and the flame azaleas
are finally beginning
to azale.

MAC COLLINS

WES BROWNE

When it was published in early January, Wes Browne's second novel *They All Fall the Same* sparked instant buzz online. The Southern noir thriller brings back Burl Spoon, a central character from Browne's 2020 debut *Hillbilly Hustle*, whose cannabis empire is still going strong in Jackson County, Kentucky after three decades. But all is not well for Spoon behind the scenes. His family is falling apart, and following two tragedies, Spoon retaliates against another drug kingpin, setting up a chilling, brutal conflict. Readers hailed the novel for its "authentic Kentucky characters" and fast-paced plot, labeling it "crime fiction at its best." In late January, Goodreads agreed, naming the novel as one of "2025's Biggest Mysteries & Thrillers."

Browne talked about the book, his love of film and his experience in the courtroom with beloved Southern author and raconteur George Singleton, whose latest book, the essay collection *Asides: Occasional Essays on Dogs, Food, Restaurants, Bars, Hangovers, Jobs, Music, Family Trees, Robbery, Relationships, Being Brought Up Questionably, Et Cetera,* was published in 2023.

■ ■ ■

GEORGE SINGLETON: It's probably bad form to compare a novel with movies, but *They All Fall the Same* has everything: *The French Connection, The Fugitive, Django Unchained, Bonnie and Clyde*, Hatfields and McCoys, even *Guess Who's Coming to Dinner*. Are there any particular movies that, looking back, may have inspired you?

WES BROWNE: The book *Winter's Bone* is a masterpiece, but I saw the movie long before I read it. My friend Mark Westmoreland has said *They All Fall the Same* is a little like *Winter's Bone* from Tear Drop's perspective. I like that idea. I do know I was influenced by it.

There's a book blogger named Scott Lovelace who posted a video about *They All Fall the Same* where he compared it to *A Time To Kill*, which I hadn't thought about, but I can see it. I didn't read the book, but I saw the movie. Maybe that was in my head a little.

I'm a huge Paul Newman fan, so there could be some Hud in there. Charisma and cruelty in one package. I didn't think to give my protagonist blue eyes.

They're in series, not movies, but two characters I love are Walter White from *Breaking Bad* and Tony Soprano from *The Sopranos*. There's no doubt in my mind I was inspired by those two characters. Both are objectively bad guys with family issues that complicate their lives, and just enough humanity in them that you hold out hope for some redemption.

GS: You're a complex man, Wes—attorney, restauranteur, and writer. Lacrosse coach, bon vivant, music lover, University of Kentucky athletics enthusiast. Do you sleep?

WB: Fitfully and not enough. I say this in all seriousness. Reading and writing help me. I've had trouble falling asleep since I was a kid because I have racing thoughts. I think about work and worries, and at this point, humanity. When I go to bed, I read until the book is falling out of my hands, then, when I finally put the book down, I think about whatever writing project I'm working on until I nod off. Something about that occupies my brain in a way that works like magic.

When I'm in the thick of writing a novel, I nap in the early evening so I can write into the late night and early morning. If you love writing, you make time for it no matter how busy you are. And I love it. It's been my passion since I was in the fourth grade. I make time for it no matter how busy I get.

Wes Browne   *Photo: Erica Chambers*

57

GS: Burl Spoon was a character in *Hillbilly Hustle*. What made you want to flesh out his story? Also, have you encountered such characters in the courtroom?

WB: Shew. Long answer. I was done with the story in *Hillbilly Hustle*, but I kept thinking about Burl and what his life looked like apart from that. He's so commanding and seemingly untouchable, but what would happen to him if he got touched? I thought about writing a character similar to him, but that didn't make any sense. I already had his rhythms down and he still fascinated me. So I wrote this new story from scratch. If you know both books, they're completely different. Aside from Burl, there's not much connecting them.

I've seen all kinds in the courtroom, but not many like Burl. Usually, if someone of his stature is brought to justice, it happens in federal court. I don't really like federal court. Too formal for me.

I initially based Burl on several people. There was a guy in a county I worked who would go see the judge before court each week, and the people he wanted to get help, were helped. Nobody questioned that. The judge he saw wound up in federal prison, by the way. There's some of that guy in Burl.

How Burl talks is based on a maintenance man I know. This guy will ask me for a favor, and if I say, "no," he'll say, "well, fuck you then," and laugh about it. That's just his way. Coarse as hell. But then he has this softer side to him that comes through now and then when he talks about his family and stuff like that. That's Burl Spoon.

Writing someone who is fundamentally not a good person, and doing it in a way that readers still pull for them, kind of epitomizes what I like to do as a writer. There's humanity and potential for redemption in just about everyone. So you have to find subtle ways to get that across without losing the character's essential nature. If I think about it, that's what I've done as a criminal defense attorney my entire adult life. Try to convince people that someone who's done something bad has potential for good in them. Burl is just another client, I guess.

GS: Crime fiction seems to be undergoing a certain renaissance. Do you have any favorite past masters of the genre? Who's at the top of their game at the moment?

WB: I was brought up on Elmore Leonard. I grew up about thirty minutes from where he lived in Michigan. My mom used to go to a lot of author events and she met him. She got him to sign me a copy of *Out of Sight*, and he wrote "Good luck with your novel" in it. I was in my early twenties, but I was already working on one. I finally published *Hillbilly Hustle* when I was forty-six, so you can see how long it took me to figure it out, but I treasured what he wrote in that book. I haven't read all of his books, but I've read most. I don't write just like him, but his influence is there.

S.A. Cosby is kind of the pinnacle of the business at the moment, and there's a reason for it. Everything he writes is gold. What's lovely about his success is, he's such a wonderful and generous guy. He gave me notes on this book that helped me and his blurb graces the cover. I get compared to him some, but I know for a fact I can't do what he does. I just try to do what I do and hope people like it.

Some other contemporary masters I admire are Jordan Harper and Megan Abbott. Those two both awe me. If you're talking more rural noir, your buddies Tom Franklin, Ron Rash, Chris Offutt, and of course, Donald Ray Pollock, are role models. And then there are my buddies, David Joy, Eli Cranor, Kelly J. Ford, and David Heska Wanbli Weiden, who are also at the top of the game. I could go on.

GS: In chapter twenty-one, Burl Spoon's son Darron says to his father, "...You belittle everyone and everything that doesn't bend to your will. Everyone's beneath you because they don't have the money and power you have. You don't bring anything to this world...And it doesn't matter how much you have to cheat so long as at the end of the day you feel like you're winning. ..." Is there any way that Trump came to mind as you wrote this? Or Napoleon (seeing as Burl is short in stature)?

WB: Not consciously, but I can see how you could draw that conclusion. The reason people don't quite turn on Burl all the way is that here and there his love for others bleeds through. Though he rarely does it, he has the capacity to put loved ones before himself, and he has some well-buried empathy in him that can be coaxed out. The other thing about Burl that is imperfect, but exists, is his love and respect for women. He's certainly no role model, but if you pay attention, it's women who coax goodness from him, it's women who elicit his most generous nature, and it's women who are his salvation.

GS: I despise myself for asking this question, but it seems to be the first question whenever there's a Q&A at a book signing/reading: Do you have a process?

WB: I come up with a beginning and an end, and then I just make stuff up until I get to the end, and the end typically is not what I thought it would be when I started. Elmore Lenoard talked about pushing his characters out the door and seeing where they go. That is probably his biggest influence on me. So my process is pretty damn loose. I don't believe in plotting in advance too much, because people's lives are built on how things play out and their reactions to that. How am I supposed to figure out all those reactions in advance if I haven't been through them with the character yet? If I do my thing the right way, you'd think I plotted the whole thing out meticulously. That's the magic. When it comes together as if I had a plan all along.

I have a very short attention span, so I'm constantly trying to build tension, conflict, and suspense, and set up lots of mini climaxes and set pieces on my way to the final climax. But a book can't be all pyrotechnics. That's actually very boring. You need stretches of quiet to make those dynamic scenes pop. You've got to do a lot of character building and story building, because if readers aren't made to care about the characters, there's no stakes in what happens to them, so that's what I do between this and that popping off. I make readers care. But each time I'm in a quieter part of the book, I'm looking ahead thinking I've got to have something sexy happen soon or I'll lose people. Hell, I'll bore myself writing it.

GS: DeeDee, Burl's daughter, succumbs to fentanyl-laced heroin. I know that your region's been plagued with meth and fentanyl, along with the rest of America. Do you think there's any hope on the horizon?

WB: I don't know. At least there's some recognition of the problem, but it's a little like plugging cracks in a dam. Another always opens up. Fentanyl is getting put in everything because it's cheap and it makes people feel good. It's like the MSG of drugs, but it can kill you so easily. People know about it being in heroin, but they're finding it in vape cartridges that are supposedly THC. People think they're getting weed, and they're getting fentanyl. That's just one example.

One place I see hope is in the emphasis on treatment over punishment for users. Users are victims themselves. Punishment without treatment is just further victimization. We need to concentrate on getting the victims well, not incarcerating them, and that's taken hold to some extent.

I didn't set out to write an "issue" book, but I made a conscious decision to write about opioids touching a family, and specifically touching a family with the money and means for treatment, and how even with that, you can lose someone. I hoped to get people to think about the scope of the problem and how it could impact them and their loved ones.

GS: I suppose *They All Fall the Same* could take place in Montana or Connecticut, but the Kentucky/Tennessee area seems perfect. I know, also, that you hail from Michigan. Talk about what Kentucky means to you when it comes to setting.

WB: I try to be really open about my background. I always joke that I don't want to be the Rachel Dolezal of Appalachian literature. I'm fifty-years-old, but I moved here when I was twenty-two to go to law school and have been immersed in the culture and the legal system since then.

For me to write this book, Kentucky was the only option. This is the place I know the best. I know people who get into the kind of trouble I write about, who have the types of relationships I write about, and who see the world in the way my characters see the world.

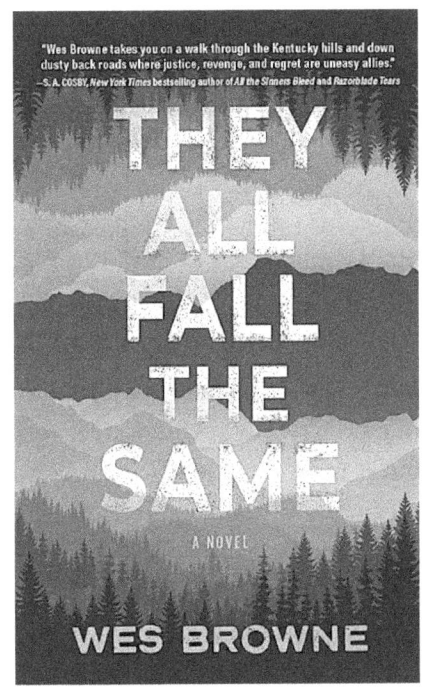

"Wes Browne takes you on a walk through the Kentucky hills and down dusty back roads where justice, revenge, and regret are uneasy allies."
—S. A. COSBY, *New York Times* bestselling author of *All the Sinners Bleed* and *Razorblade Tears*

THEY ALL FALL THE SAME

A NOVEL

WES BROWNE

I've traveled all over the region practicing law. When I go different places, I like to hang around, eat in local restaurants, go to convenience stores and junk stores, and talk to people. Then there's the courthouses. I've spent hours on end in back rooms killing time with other attorneys, courthouse staff, police officers, defendants, judges, just shooting the breeze. Add to that what I've seen and heard in jails. I could write about somewhere else, and I do, but right now, Kentucky and Kentucky characters come the most naturally.

GS: There are strong, three-dimensional women in this novel: Colleen, DeeDee, Whitney, even granddaughter Chelsea. I remember in old, old crime novels, sometimes the female characters were treated as an aside. While you were writing, did you say, "I have to make the women in this novel stronger/more rational/more sympathetic than the men in their lives?"

WB: One reason I don't love all of the crime classics is because the way women are written in some of them is pretty terrible. They show up, they're thinly-sketched props, and they go to bed with the protagonist, or they get murdered, or both. It's all so predictable, and it panders to readers' worst natures. Fortunately, the genre is headed to a better place, and we're seeing less of that.

And yes, I did try to make the key women in this book more virtuous and rational than the men, because in my experience, it's so often true. So I think it's realistic. There are some women in the book who are less so, but I didn't dwell on them much. Burl is a man who is allowed to exist, and who thrives, in a negative way due to the complicity and acquiescence of other men. It's mostly the women in his life who stand up to him, who demand better of him, and who ultimately preserve his humanity.

GS: What's next?

WB: I'm doing what I like to call my "Elmore Leonard pivot." I've already published two novels set in Kentucky that are very much books of this region. My next one I went somewhere completely different, like Leonard did, but I anchored it in my own background and researched the hell out of it.

It's a fish-out-of-water book about a former Michigan State Police sharpshooter recruit who becomes disenchanted after his sister passes away, quits the academy, and moves to Las Vegas where he joins a high-end theft ring. Eventually he sours on that as well, ends up flipping on his co-conspirators, lands on probation, falls in love, violates his probation, crosses a crime boss, and ends up on the run from hitmen, the law, and a guard from a women's prison who hates him. The working title is *Twenty-Nine Palms Highway.* ■

PULLING IN

Remember the turn that woke
something in us to say we were

almost home? Is this the same ache
as late September, that same, familiar door

abandoned train-tracks whisper towards?
And what about woodsmoke, mist

over the cow pond, words? Is all of it
just pebbles on the one, gravel

drive? I've been on this road
long enough to know not to ask

if we're there yet, but no one can stop
the signs from saying we're getting closer.

And you, behind the wheel up there,
face flickering in and out

of our blurry sight in the dim light
of street lamps, your occasional whispers

veiled behind the gritty static of AM
radio, just know that I'm half-awake

back here and can't walk straight,
so you'll absolutely need to carry me in.

LUKE HARVEY

A-TO-B

What's crumpled in the glove box
won't show you where you are,

no red star to make clear
You Are Here. What it *can* offer,

though, is a survey of the scene,
complete with county lines, free-

ways, and other scars that remain
more or less unchanging with time.

It's up to you to find the gnarled tree,
the engine shop, the places

that place us in-between.
With enough attention you might

even drop a tentative pin,
and then another, and given—as we

might suspect—a few wrong turns,
take out a pen and begin

the slow work of mapping
the chasm between the two.

LUKE HARVEY

BULLFROG

HEATHER SWAIN

Laurel woke up knowing something was wrong. She had gone to bed feverish after playing in the river with the kids, but this was more than a little fever. A sense of dread crept up the back of her neck and settled in her throat like a frog that she couldn't clear. She thought through possibilities.

Her children? Last she checked, Jax and Cady were both asleep in the next room of the cabin. Had one or both of them stopped breathing? Carbon monoxide? The CO monitor hadn't gone off, so poisoning was unlikely.

Her parents? She'd spoken to them earlier that day. They were spending Thanksgiving with her brother Eric in Spokane. Then again, people die after big meals sometimes. That happened to her friend Carla. When she was home for Thanksgiving her junior year of college, her father felt a tightness in his chest but insisted it was only heartburn. Then he keeled over at the dinner table, mashed potatoes still on his fork. Carla performed CPR while her mother and sister shrieked and wept. By the time the ambulance arrived, her father was as dead as the turkey carcass on the table.

If one of Laurel's parents had keeled over, Eric would let her know. Plus, there was nothing she could do about it anyway, so for now she'd operate under the assumption that her parents were fine.

Had she heard a weird noise? She strained to listen beyond her husband Avery's labored breathing. She rolled over and stared out the window. A light fog shrouded the night sky, making the moon merely a suggestion through the gauzy curtains. Beyond Avery, she could hear the faint but familiar sounds of the North Carolina woods. Night creatures rustled. Crickets chirped. Cicadas whirled. Somewhere, a sly red fox scurried through dry leaves while a black bear lumbered through the brambles. She could just make out the deep bellow from a bullfrog—maybe the one she'd pulled out of the mud that day. If frogs held grudges like Avery, then the bullfrog probably went to bed mad at her, too.

She rolled onto her other hip and faced Avery's back. Maybe her shenanigans in the river had caused some nefarious force to slither through the woods and into the cabin unnoticed to steal one or both of her children away. She shook herself and rolled onto her back. That was the stuff of fantasy and science fiction. Laurel prided herself on being logical and straightforward. A problem solver. She was a lawyer with a husband and two kids, for god's sake. She was in the place she loved most in the world—her Papaw's cabin the woods. Lying awake with an irrational sense of doom like a dark cloud obscuring the moon was stupid, she told herself.

Maybe it was too quiet. Maybe she was becoming too much of a New Yorker like Avery. In Brooklyn, he could sleep through garbage trucks, fire engines, and bar brawls that spilled onto the sidewalk, but out in the woods, any little noise could send him bolt upright like a mummy rising from the dead—which is why she lay there, heat pooling in her face, heart pounding as if she'd run rather than get up. Avery thought her jaunt in the river and this fever were connected. Laurel did not want to give him the satisfaction of being right.

"You can't get dengue fever from the Watauga River," she'd told him, but he was skeptical of the woods. He checked the kids for ticks every time they stepped foot back inside the cabin.

"It's probably a virus," she'd said. And this made sense because with two young children, illnesses marched through their family like ants across a sticky kitchen countertop. Someone always had a runny nose, a little cough, a rash, itchy eyes. Each time, Avery wanted to call the pediatrician, but Laurel never did. "They're building up their immunity," she insisted, because her summers in North Carolina as a child had made her more robust than her husband and she wanted her children to be rugged like her.

She'd spent her summers running wild through the woods with her brother, their cousins, and a local boy named Ben Atkins. He'd been a scrawny, sunburnt kid with a cowlick in the center of his forehead and a smattering of freckles across the bridge of his nose. His smile was marked by a crooked canine and a dimple on his left cheek. Until the summer when they were fifteen, when she found that he had blossomed into an Adonis, over six-feet tall with the build of a swimmer—broad-shouldered, narrow-hipped—and darker, sandy hair that had grown out in soft waves which he continually shook out of his face to reveal the fading freckles. That was the summer she fell madly in love with Ben.

She'd only been back in Boone for twenty-four hours, but the cabin stirred up so many memories. Each time she glanced into the tree line, she'd remember a former version of herself traipsing through the woods with Ben on her heels. Part of her wanted to run after that phantom girl, tap her on the shoulder and see if they'd recognize each other after so long apart. Instead, she'd coaxed the twins into the river with her as proof of who she used to be in these woods.

She'd only been back in Boone for twenty-four hours, but the cabin stirred up so many memories. Each time she glanced into the tree line, she'd remember a former version of herself traipsing through the woods with Ben on her heels.

Avery had wanted the kids to wear life jackets.

Laurel rolled her eyes. "The water is barely above their ankles."

"What if there's a flash flood and they get swept away?" Avery asked from his spot on the bank. He wore socks with sandals to protect his feet from ticks.

Laurel had an urge to push him in the river, just for fun. She and Ben used to do that. A stupid game that always made her laugh. When one of them least expected it—BAM!

In they'd go. Of course, she didn't push her husband. She maintained her composure. Yet some part of her still felt like a half-feral teenager who wanted nothing more than to kick off her shoes, shimmy out of her cut-offs, and jump in the river to float on her back, holding hands with Ben so they wouldn't drift apart until she had to go back home in the fall. She had been more brazen during those summers. More full of possibilities. Now she felt scrunched, like a flower that had once bloomed, then was squeezed back into its bud.

But the river freed her.

While wading in the water with the kids, she heard the frog's call like low notes on a cello among a symphony of bird song.

Jax stood up tall to listen. "Mommy, is that a monster?"

Cady wrapped her arms around Laurel's leg and stamped her feet in the water.

Laurel rubbed circles on Cady's back, but refused to pick her up. "It's just a big old bullfrog," she told the girls. "Listen." They were quiet and waited for the frog's bellow. It came again, like a slack guitar string being plucked. Laurel laughed, delighted.

"How big is it?" Jax asked, eyes wide.

"Well, my papaw taught me that the deeper the bellow, the bigger the frog. So this one sounds sort of medium-sized. Like a bagel. You want to meet him?"

Cady looked up at her, unsure. "We can meet a frog?"

"Sure can. That bullfrog is a friend of mine," Laurel chuckled, because this was the kind of nonsense her papaw would have peddled and here she was, doing the same silly thing. "I bet he'll hop right into my hands if we can find him."

Avery sighed. "You're not really going to pick up a bullfrog, are you?"

"Why wouldn't I?" she asked. If she'd been joking before, now she was determined.

"They carry diseases, like salmonella," he said.

"That's turtles," she told him. "From a tank. In pet shops. Not out here. These guys are harmless." She picked up a stick from the river's edge to part the tall sedges.

They heard a ribbit, then a loud plop. "He just jumped in the water," she whispered to the kids. "Come on."

She took Jax's and Cady's hands and the three of them moved slowly and quietly across the shallows, their feet sucked down by the soft riverbed. Laurel loved the mud oozing between her bare toes, but of course the kids had on water shoes thanks to Avery. (No socks, thanks to her.) She threaded the stick through the reeds near the bank where she'd heard the plop and there it was, a big old bullfrog blinking up at them.

As soon as it saw them, the frog pivoted away, pumping its legs to propel itself back toward shore. But Laurel was quick. As she'd learned to do as a child, she lunged and reached out ahead of the frog, exactly where it would hop onto shore. It was in her hands before she even realized it. She wasn't sure who was more surprised—the kids, the frog, or herself.

"Hello, bullfrog," she said. Its back legs paddled at the air while it tried to pry itself loose from her grip with its fat front toes. "Don't worry, fella, we just want to say hi."

Cady and Jax stood in awe, eyes wide, mouths open like little spring peepers. "Want to touch him?" Laurel asked.

"Absolutely not!" Avery bellowed from the shore.

Normally, Laurel had more patience for Avery's reticence about nature, but he was being such a stick in the mud and ruining her fun that she exploded, "Oh, come on!" She took a breath and tried to soften. "There's nothing wrong with this fella, see?" She lifted the frog up to her face and kissed it on the head.

"Mommy!" Jax yelled. "You kissed the frog!"

"Maybe it'll turn into a prince." Laurel smirked at Avery, hoping to tease him out of his snit, but he just huffed at her from the shore.

Cady squealed and held out her hands. "I want to hold it!"

Laurel didn't want to provoke a fight with Avery in front of the kids so she said, "Let's just say hello for now so we don't scare our new friend."

"Hello, froggy," Cady whispered and waved. "Hello."

"Do you girls know the parable of the boiling frog?" Avery asked.

"What's a parable?" Jax asked.

"A story with a lesson," Avery said.

"Avery, stop." Laurel stroked the frog's back with her thumb. She loved the smooth skin and its plumpness in her hands. She could feel its heart beating and see its pulse behind its bulging eyes.

Avery barreled ahead. "If you put a frog in a pot of hot water, it'll jump out, but if you put it in a pot of cool water and slowly turn up the heat..."

The frog squirmed and pushed against her fingers, trying to pry itself loose.

"...the frog will get too comfortable and won't notice that the temperature is rising until..." he paused for effect, and then he boomed, "it boils to death!"

Cady and Jax burst into tears.

"Nice going," Laurel hissed at Avery. She turned to the kids. "We're not going to hurt the frog. We're going to let it go. Okay? Now say bye-bye." Cady and Jax sniffed and waved to the frog. Laurel crouched down and gingerly set the creature in a stand of sedge so it could disappear from them with dignity.

"Come on," Avery said. "Let's go. Everybody out. That's enough nature for the day." He held out his hands to pull Jax and Cady onto the bank. They ran ahead on the path toward the cabin.

"Oh, for God's sake, Avery," Laurel said as she trudged out of the water. "We were having fun."

"Yeah, that frog was having a great time," he sniped.

"Parable of the frog?" Laurel shook her head, disgusted. "It probably heard you and was like, *Fuck you buddy, we'd hop out, you're the ones stupid enough to stay in boiling water.*"

Avery snorted. "It's probably being eaten by a great blue heron right now."

"Shows what you know. That frog is way too big to be eaten by a heron," she told him, even though she wasn't sure that was true.

Avery just shrugged. "Are you going to give the girls a bath, or should I?"

"It wasn't my idea to pull them out of the river," Laurel said.

"So you'd let them go to bed like that?"

Laurel shrugged. "Never hurt me."

"Well, at least wash your hands when you come inside, for god's sake."

The urge to push Avery into the river pulsed through Laurel's body. Telling her to wash her hands? She wanted to lick her palms in front of him. But of course, she wouldn't do it, nor would she push him. Mostly because he wouldn't budge. Unlike Ben, who was always loose and distracted, Avery had a vigilance about him. He'd never let his guard down enough to be shoved. When they were in New York, Avery's personality fit. She felt protected from the chaos of the city when she was with him. No one was going to fuck with her and the girls. But in Boone? He was whiny, petulant, and annoyed with her all the time.

"I'm not ready to come inside," Laurel said.

"Suit yourself," said Avery as he marched up the path.

Laurel put on the sneakers she'd kicked off earlier and walked the opposite way, deeper into the woods. She stomped through the undergrowth beneath tall pines and oaks. How could anyone have enough nature for a day? What a stupid thing to say. And the whole boiling frog story? Idiotic. What kind of person tells that to children?

She stopped and placed her hand against the sturdy trunk of a giant tree that had likely been here when her grandfather was a boy. She leaned into the tree and wondered if she could stay there long enough to root into its bark like the moss growing up the north side. She gazed up at the leaves. Maple— five-fingered hands. They were just beginning to change

She leaned into the tree and wondered if she could stay there long enough to root into its bark like the moss growing up the north side. She gazed up at the leaves.

color even though it was late November. Climate change was delaying autumn bit by bit each year. Winters hardly snowed anymore. She felt an urgency to get as much time as possible with the kids in these woods before everything went to hell.

Laurel saw a young sassafras tree up ahead. She'd know it anywhere. Her papaw had taught them to identify the tree by its three distinct leaves—one ovate, one mitten-shaped with a thumb sticking out, and one three-lobed, like a hand with a pinky on one side and a thumb on the other. She reached out and crushed a yellow-thumbed leaf between her fingers. The sweet, citrusy scent transported her straight back to childhood, tramping behind Papaw on paths only he could see. He was tall and lanky, always dressed in greens and browns, like the forest come to life. And this made her feel safe, as if no harm could come to her when she was in the woods. He used to dig up sassafras roots to make tea. Avery would shit a brick if she brought home a shriveled dirty root to boil up. This thought made her laugh.

Maybe she was being vindictive, but part of her wanted to do it anyway. Maybe she wanted Avery to see her fully for who she was. As the saying went, you can take the girl out of the woods, but you can't take the woods out of the girl. So she set to digging.

Of course, Avery was livid when she brought a chunk of sassafras root into the house. It had taken a lot of effort to wrestle it out of the ground and she was filthy. He was nearly apoplectic when she tracked dirt into the cabin then scrubbed down the root in the sink and tossed it in a pot of boiling water.

"What the actual hell are you doing?" he growled at her while the kids worked an ancient jigsaw puzzle at the kitchen table.

"I'm making Papaw's sassafras tea!"

"You are not seriously going to drink that?" he said, jabbing his finger toward the reddish-brown water bubbling on the stove.

"People have been drinking this for thousands of years. Native Americans and colonists and everyone in my family," Laurel said proudly, even though it likely wasn't true.

"Mmm," Jax said. "I smell root beer."

"That's right," Laurel told her. "This is natural root beer."

"I want to try some," Cady said.

"Absolutely not," Avery barked.

Laurel and Avery stared hard at one another. Sometimes their fights would last for days. She knew if she pushed further, it could take the rest of the trip to reach a détente. Besides, she knew it was more important to him that the girls didn't drink the tea than it was to her that they did, so she relented. "Daddy's right," she said and turned to find a spoon. "This isn't a drink for kids."

She stirred the pot but couldn't bring herself to toss the whole brew out, so she scooped up a bit of liquid and blew away the steam. "But Mommy's going to have some." She locked eyes with Avery as she sipped. "Yum," she said, even though it mostly tasted like dirt.

Now, hours later, she sat on the edge of the bed with her feet dangling toward the floor and the taste of dirt still in her throat. She tried to swallow it down but a wave of nausea passed over her and she wondered if she had dug up the wrong root and got a hold of something poisonous. She pretended to be some kind of country girl. In truth, she hadn't spent the summer in North Carolina for nearly twenty years. But come on. One tiny taste of tea and one little kiss on a bullfrog's head couldn't make her this sick. And yet she felt slick and swollen. Her fingers felt fat, and her throat and neck felt thick. She eased herself off the bed, thinking a warm bath might help.

In the bathroom, she fumbled for the light switch then looked at herself in the mirror. Her eyes were puffy and both lips were plump. Her fingers looked as fat as the hot dogs the kids had eaten for dinner. She knew something was really wrong. She rifled through the medicine cabinet and under the sink and found nothing but old Band-Aids and half a tube of Neosporin. She was probably having an allergic reaction, but there were no antihistamines in sight. She thought for a moment about calling an ambulance, but quickly dismissed the idea. The EMTs would never find the dirt road, and even if they did, they'd have trouble getting down the hill and back up again.

She padded silently to the bedroom and hovered in the doorway. Avery snored loudly. If she woke him, he would freak out. They'd have to rouse the kids and all pile in the car.

Worse, he'd never stop gloating that he was right about the dangers of nature. She'd rather drive herself to the ER than risk that outcome, so she headed for the back door. She knew the way to the hospital. She had the car. She would be there quick.

Laurel had plenty of practice sneaking out of the cabin in the middle of the night to meet Ben when she was a teenager. The back door barely made a noise if she turned the handle slowly. She knew not to let the screen door slam and how to walk in the grass to avoid crunching gravel. With a hybrid, she didn't even have to push the car in neutral to get past the house before she turned it on.

As Laurel drove up the steep hill to the main road, she could feel a tingling in the back of her throat as if her neck was shortening and her head was drawing down toward her shoulders. At the top of the hill, she hit the pavement. Six miles to the ER. Less than fifteen minutes. She could make it if she just stayed calm and focused on the twisting road shrouded in fog.

Her hands automatically moved the wheel left and right for each curve. Ben's family had lived at the other end of town in an A-frame cabin in the woods. He always smelled of pine. She passed a picnic area where they used to lie back on the tables, looking up at the stars, dreaming aloud what their lives would be in the future. He'd gotten in to UNC in Chapel Hill. She was going to Duke like her mother. They'd only be an hour apart, so they would stay together. He would become a veterinarian. She'd study anthropology and they'd travel the world, then settle down on a goat farm in the Smoky Mountains with four tow-headed kids.

She passed the hazy lights of the town high school. She and Ben had broken up on the abandoned bleachers before the end of her last summer here. She couldn't remember why, just that he'd put his hand on her cheek to wipe away tears she didn't want to cry. When Laurel left for college, she filed him away under "first love," then let herself lose track of him. Until she came back to Boone and he reanimated in her mind.

How childish the whole thing seemed now, but still, the intensity of the memories nearly took her breath away. She tried to take long deep breaths like the doula taught her for labor, but her throat and chest felt too tight. She had the urge to scream, but that too felt stuck, as if she needed more space in her body—an extra pouch or a sac—to hold all the feelings being back here had stirred up.

She glanced at herself in the rearview mirror. Her eyes were hooded. Her face was rounder. Her breathing had become raspier. In the murky light of the hidden moon, her skin looked greenish and mottled. She stared at her hands gripping the steering wheel. They, too, were fat and blotchy. She thought of the bullfrog trying to push itself out of her grip. She understood its need for escape. Part of her wanted to pull the car over, abandon it by the side of the road, and dart into the dark woods. And then what? Burrow down into the mud, waiting for some transformation that would absolve her of the life she'd picked when she left this place?

No. Laurel drove on.

She pulled in front of the ER and spilled out of the car. Her tongue was fat in her mouth. Every breath was a gasp. Her feet felt heavy. Her legs bowed as if her hips had splayed on the drive. She wanted to put her hands on the ground to hop inside but she forced herself to stay upright.

Inside the ER, through the slits of her eyes, she could make out a man in blue scrubs asleep behind a plexiglass window. His head was tipped back, his mouth half open, his orange Crocs propped up on the desk. She tried to speak, but nothing came out. She tapped on the glass. The man bolted awake. Laurel put one hand to her throat and croaked.

Immediately, he had her on a gurney. Something sharp jabbed her thigh. A great blue heron's beak pulling her from warm, murky water into the bright, cold light of day. She flailed and tried to fight. She tried to puff up her vocal sac to bellow.

The man in blue scrubs bent close to her ear as he put a mask over her nose and mouth. "I'm taking you into triage. The epinephrine will kick in soon," he told her. "Try to breathe."

Laurel's heart raced and her body shook, but the pain in her thigh subsided. The heron had let go. She pulled in a long, deep breath, then dove into the safety of the dark river to swim away.

Sometime later, Laurel swam up again. She fought her way to the surface and opened her eyes to see orange Crocs

Laurel's heart raced and her body shook, but the pain in her thigh subsided. The heron had let go. She pulled in a long, deep breath, then dove into the safety of the dark river to swim away.

propped up on her bed. The man in scrubs sat beside her. "Hey there, you're real pretty now that you're not all swole up like a bullfrog," he said in a deep Southern drawl.

What the fuck century did I land in? Laurel thought, suddenly clear-headed. She blinked at him. Then blinked again. A jolt of recognition hit her. "Ben?" she barked.

"Hey there, Laur." He stood up and dropped the goofy accent. "I didn't recognize you at first. That was quite a reaction you had there." He grimaced.

She pulled the oxygen mask off her face. "Wait." She sat up to get a better look. Her heart fluttered, though she wasn't sure if that was from the epinephrine or from the jolt of seeing Ben Atkins in person. "Is that really you? Am I hallucinating?"

"It's me." He smiled. Same crooked canine she'd always found endearing. Same dimple on his left cheek she used to kiss. Same thick sandy hair with a cowlick she always ran her fingers through after they swam. He sat next to her on the bed, and she had the urge to pull him close and smell his piney essence to make sure it was really Ben, but of course she didn't.

"What are you doing here? I thought you left Boone," she said. "UNC? Chapel Hill?"

He shrugged. "Got as far as Appalachian State..." He trailed off, pointing toward the campus on the northwest side of town.

"And...you're a doctor?" Laurel tried to reconcile where their lives had jumped off the timeline they'd laid down for one another the summer they turned eighteen.

"Nurse," he said. "I heard you live in New York."

"I do," she said. "But we bought Papaw's cabin when he passed."

He nodded. "I heard something about that, too. Who's we?"

"Husband, two girls. Twins," she explained and felt blood rise to her cheeks at the thought of Avery and their beautiful dark-haired children. "You?" she asked and braced herself. What did she want him to say? He'd never loved again? Or he was wildly happy without her? Neither would be satisfying.

"Same," he said with a shrug and a smile. "Only a wife and two boys for me."

"Who'd you marry? Do I know her?" Laurel perked up as possibilities of Ben's wife zipped through her mind. Petite and perky? Long-legged hippie? Was she into crystals? Could she bale hay and make pickles?

"She's not from around here. And, she's my soon-to-be-ex-wife," he clarified, then held up his hands as if to say, *what can you do?*

At the sound of *ex*, Laurel felt a pang deep in her belly—a mix of fear and excitement—like the impulse to jump into the rapids of the deep, cold river, but she stayed put.

"You were in bad shape when you bumbled in," Ben said, and then he squeezed her thigh just above the knee. If it had been anyone else, the gesture would have been different. Reassurance? Kindness? Compassion? But Ben's hand on her leg felt more like the reclamation of a body he'd once known well. "What happened?" he asked.

She shook her head. Tears leaked out of the corners of her eyes only she wasn't sure why.

"Hey, hey. It's okay. You're okay. I got you." Ben wiped away her tears with his thumb. Same thing he'd done when they broke up. Now here he was again, and Laurel felt the dissonance of all possible Laurels between then and now.

The Laurel who had stayed here with her first love instead of leaving for college. The one who dropped out of Duke to join the Peace Corps instead of finishing her degree. The one who'd married her British boyfriend and lived in London instead of moving to New York alone. The one who'd said no to Avery's proposal, even though she was sick of dating in her thirties in an unfamiliar city. The one who'd returned to her grandfather's land and transformed into a frog, then hopped away to live a different life in the woods.

She grabbed Ben's wrist and held it tight. "I was a frog, wasn't I?" she whispered.

Ben laughed. It was the same laugh as when they were kids, but now there were lines around his eyes, only on him they were rays of sun and not wrinkles. "Well, you sure didn't look like yourself, but..."

"Then what the fuck was it?" she asked. It came out angry. She needed him to be different than Avery, who'd roll his eyes at the slightest suggestion of transmogrification. She needed

Ben to understand that the woods were trying to reclaim her and she might want to acquiesce.

"Well…the medical explanation would be anaphylaxis," he said seriously and patted her hand. "Your throat swelled up. And you were probably hallucinating. Did you eat something weird?"

She hung her head, embarrassed to admit, "I made sassafras tea from a root." How stupid she had been! How cavalier! Her grandfather had always advised her not to mess with the woods unless she knew what she was messing with. "But I know it was sassafras! Papaw made it for us all the time."

Ben shrugged. "Could have been something in the dirt. A bacteria. A fungus. Who knows. It happens sometimes," he assured her, then he let it go. "Who's here with you? Want me to bring your hubby in?"

"I drove myself," she told Ben.

"You drove yourself to the hospital in the middle of anaphylactic shock?"

"I didn't know it was anaphylaxis! And I didn't want to wake everybody up and…"

Ben guffawed. "Same old Laurel!"

"What's that supposed to mean?"

"Stubborn. Pig-headed. Going to do things your way or no way and not get help from anybody."

"I'm not *that* bad."

"Ha!" Ben snorted, but he grinned at her, full of delight. "You had our whole lives planned out! Duke for you. UNC for me."

"You wanted those things, too!" she exclaimed, but Ben just shook his head.

"I never could keep up with you. You were always three steps ahead. I asked you to stay, but…"

Laurel felt slapped. *Asked her to stay?* She had no recollection of that.

"Even then, I knew you wouldn't," Ben continued. "You were always in the river before I could get there. And if I ever beat you, you'd shove me in then laugh your ass off."

Laurel knew every word of what he said was true. She had wanted to pull Ben out of this place and take him with her into the wider world. And when he refused to go, she left without him.

"Those days were sure fun, though," Ben chuckled. "Is life in New York fun?"

Laurel looked down at her hands. They were hers again. "Sometimes," she said.

"You happy?" he asked, more seriously.

Laurel thought this over for a moment. When they bought Papaw's cabin, she had a whisper of a plan to come back and replant her roots. Now, here she was, face to face with the biggest part of her past who had his hand on her thigh, telling her about his soon-to-be ex-wife. Yet six miles up the windy road, Jax and Cady slept with Avery as their protector. No nefarious forces could slither in to get them as long as he was there.

"Happy enough, I suppose," she said. Then she shook her head and looked up at the ceiling. "Or maybe I'm too dumb to notice that the water is coming to a boil."

Ben snorted. "Life's like that. But, whatcha gonna do? Hop off into the river?"

"And get eaten by a heron?" she asked.

"Want me to call somebody to come get you? One of your cousins? Or..." he looked at his watch. "I'm off in an hour. I can drive you back." He raised his eyebrows.

Laurel opened her mouth to say yes, but then she paused and studied Ben Atkins. In that moment, she saw the full timeline of his life etched across his features, from squirrelly kid to Adonic teen to mellow aging man, and somewhere in the center of that line was a dot marked *Laurel*. The question was, did she want to go back there? Could she go back there? What would it mean if she did? She wasn't ready to answer that question just yet so she said, "Nah, I can drive myself. But, god, it's really good to see you. I hope…"

"Yeah," he jumped in. "Good to see you, too. Now that you have the cabin, maybe we can, you know, get the kids together the next time you're down." He patted her leg again which sent a shiver of joy up her thigh that landed squarely below her pelvis.

"Yeah," Laurel said. "That would be nice. I want to teach my girls how to swim in the river, not in a city pool." She beamed and imagined bringing them back for the summer. Avery could stay in New York. And she could call Ben and they would get their families together. And maybe, just maybe, she'd stay. And raise her girls down here. On a goat farm. With Ben. There were so many lives one could live. To choose just one seemed unfair.

"I can tell them how I saved your life," Ben teased.

"Cocky bastard," Laurel said with a smirk and they were right back where they'd been as kids. She shoved him so hard that he fell off the bed, laughing. "You're the one who hasn't changed. Still never ready."

She felt a fire blaze up in her and found the bravado of the Laurel who used to roam the woods with him, who then went off to college alone and finished law school and moved to New York and married a man who was sometimes tough to love.

"I saved my own life," she told Ben with a laugh. "Drove my own ass here. You were asleep out there. I had to tap on the glass to wake you up."

"Oh, yeah?" Ben said. "Who hit you with an EpiPen and put that oxygen mask on your face?"

"I could have done it myself."

Ben threw his head back and laughed. "Yep," he said. "Same as ever."

Laurel liked hearing that, even if it wasn't true.

Back at the cabin, Laurel crept in as quietly as she had left. First, she checked the girls. She loved their little sleeping bodies. Jax always kicked the covers off and threw her stuffed animals on the floor. Laurel pulled the blanket over her sturdy body. Wisps of dark brown hair stuck to Cady's sweaty forehead. Laurel brushed them away then bent down to kiss each child gently and inhale their lavender soap scent. They murmured and rolled toward one another.

In their bedroom, Avery was on his side, facing the wall, no longer snoring. Laurel slid beneath the covers and faced

Same as ever, Ben had said. But he had been wrong about one thing. She had been a frog. She knew it. These woods had the power to change her if she let them.

the door. Then the thoughts began to loop. *She'd been in anaphylactic shock. What if she hadn't woken up in time? What if she hadn't made it to the hospital? What if the EpiPen hadn't worked?* Making that tea had been reckless. Drinking it was prideful. Worse, her bravado could have hurt her children if Avery hadn't been there.

Same as ever, Ben had said. But he had been wrong about one thing. She had been a frog. She knew it. These woods had the power to change her if she let them.

Avery rolled over and heaved himself her way. He slung an arm around her waist and pulled her back against his body. "There you are," he whispered.

This was the way they always forgave one another—in bed, at night, once they were both calm. She wanted to fight it.

Wrench away and puff herself up because if she could just keep the vitriol pumping, she'd have the possibility of hopping away.

"Where'd you go?" he whispered. "I was worried."

Laurel braced herself. She knew if she confessed there would be recriminations, blame, a dissection of her bad choices—the river, the frog, the tea, driving herself to a hospital in the middle of the night, her old boyfriend saving her life. They'd never split their time between Brooklyn and Boone if she told Avery everything. She'd never get to teach her daughters how to swim in the river, which was more than she could bear.

"Laurel, you okay?" Avery asked. He hugged her closer.

The emotions of that night, that day, of all the years from Ben to Avery boiled up inside of her—desire, fear, regret, love, anger, disappointment, hope. It was too much to be contained by one small human body. She felt a swelling between her chin and sternum as if the thin membrane holding everything in place was expanding. She thought she might scream so loud her voice would reverberate through the cabin walls, into the woods, and echo out across the river to be answered by the frog she'd held that day.

Only she didn't.

She swallowed it all down and held her breath as she understood that the difference between herself and a frog in a pot was that she would get to make a choice. And the truth was, she was tired and it was comfortable snuggled into Avery with her hips against his lap and his sternum against her spine. The version of her who left Boone for a life in New York was more careful, more guarded, more responsible than the girl who'd summered here.

"Everything is okay," she whispered and patted Avery's hand.

The children would sleep through the night. They would play closer to the house tomorrow. They would come back in the spring and learn to swim in the river with life jackets on. She would occasionally wave to Ben from across the grocery store parking lot. She was a lawyer with a husband and two children, for god's sake. So she closed her eyes and let herself sink down into the slowly warming water. ■

WAITING ROOM

The story goes that my wife,
just before they wheeled me back,
asked the surgeons to perform
a quick vasectomy once
they'd finished with my tumor.

Not a bad deal: two for one,
value added, and besides
there was a whole football team
of these folks, all of them good
with a knife or so you'd think.

I'm told they laughed politely.
So did she. Some grim humor
before leaving for separate
tasks, hers the hardest by far:
to sit there and do nothing

for ten or twelve nerve-wracked hours,
waiting for your love's return,
thinking about all those knives,
everything changed for good and
who knows if the joke's on you?

EVAN GURNEY

CONTRAPASSO FOR THE BRAIN DAMAGED

My guide, Virgil in a polo shirt,
takes me to the Hell Room,
a dark forest of checkerboard:

keep your eyes fixed on this point,
he says, now shake your head,
think about all the things you want

to say no to, so I look left then right,
cautiously at first but he orders
me to speed up, and now he's turned

on strobe lights that are dancing
across a sea of boxes as I try
not to fall over while standing

on one foot, and I try not to throw
up in my mouth, and I try even harder
not to shout curses at my therapist

because I know he's making me dizzy
on purpose to build new neural
networks since my nerve won't work,

and I ought to appreciate this paradox,
treating vertigo by inducing vertigo,
contrapasso for the brain damaged,

but really all this black and white
gives me is a damned headache,
and I want to ask God himself

if I did something to deserve this,
while I shake my head at the wall,
can you give me my life back,

will I ever be the same, can you
take me through hell to paradise,
but I just keep shaking my head.

EVAN GURNEY

THE RAINBOW TROUT

The sky,
a blue haze at dusk, at dawn

your grandma's homemade biscuits
spread with fresh strawberry preserves,

honeysuckle and wild raspberry juice
paint your nails the way you crave

green blades itching between your toes,
dance alongside shallow creeks

like the rainbow trout looks for crawdads
the way your father taught you,

stare in fear at their brown pincers open and
close the door to your downstairs room

try on your mother's heels
you stole from her closet, prance around

breaking beans on warm summer nights
crickets hum and lightning bugs

sparkle inside a large mason jar
a glowing orb on your nightstand, you pray

your father carries you out into the freezing cold
wrapped in your favorite blanket

underneath decaying red oak,
black gum, sugar maples

he lets you sleep while he waits
for white-tailed deer.

MIKEY JONES

BREATHE.

Take it slow. You got this
        my father whispers
into my ear

I pull
        the metal trigger
the rifle

kicks my shoulder
        into his arms
proud green eyes

fueled with adrenaline,
        we drag the doe
half a mile, back to camp

her soft coat
        mangled
                wet leaves, small twigs

      scratch her tender face

my father pierces
        a large hook
into her neck

silver chains clink
        we hoist her
                into the air

he grabs
        his large knife,
teaches me how

to slice around
        her slender throat
peel the skin back
                slowly

break the back legs
        a piercing snap
together

both hands
        gripping a tuft of fur
yank the skin off

flies swarm along
        braided intestines
dark blood pools

underneath
        a bed of purple ice
fresh meat tossed

inside a white cooler
        only a distorted
carcass left swinging.

I repeatedly scrub
           my numb hands
                    under a low water spigot

my father bends down
             beside me
in his camouflage cargo pants

hands dripping

            he gently brushes

                        bright blood

      onto my cheeks.

MIKEY JONES

AMERICAN SONNET IN THE TIME OF A WAR, NOT OUR OWN

The doctor asks *am I a patient*
Or a person, asking other doctors
Who are being people, not doctors.
She asks them if they are also patients,
Those doctors, or if they are like her,
Which makes them all people, a people
Who aren't patients when they aren't doctors,
Not now or not yet, if they are themselves
And she is herself and what's wrong is outside
Of her. As if she doesn't breathe, the world
Taken inside of her and held, each second
Since she was born; that first cry defining
A reason to keep crying, the nuclear loss
Of the amnion's pretense, being unbreachable.

DAISY BASSEN

WV MUSCLE MEMORY

I always put the emergency brake on
when I park the car. My husband
raised by the flat corn fields
of Illinois, rolls his eyes
when I've been the last to drive.
Fair enough, our city parking space
is level ground, but in West Virginia
everything's on an incline.
You've got to dig in your heels,
brace your core or you'll lose
balance. I've been gone for years
but still pitch forward
when I walk, like I'm going uphill.
When you're from somewhere
that's all slopes, you get good
at algebra quick. Calculate the possibilities
of trouble hidden around the bend.
Crave support, yearn for ballast.
Crank the hand brake.

CARRIE CONNERS

THE CALL
IS COMING FROM INSIDE THE HOUSE

MAKAYLA DANIELLE GAY

I've seen *Rosemary's Baby* twice now. At first, I understood it as a horror movie because of the telltale presence of the devil and of nosey neighbors who ask for the price of things. After watching it again, I felt the horror coming from inside the house. That is, inside the body. The true terror isn't when Mia Farrow finds the thin shimmering lines of a plot connecting herbs, doctors, neighbors, and curses to her safety. It's at the end when she's in that beautiful nightgown. She realizes there's something wrong with the baby's eyes. It wasn't just everyone around her conspiring against her unborn child, it was someone inside her too.

I was falling asleep at the end of the movie. I was coming into week two of hormone injections to make the eggs in my ovaries as snatchable as possible. The fertility doctor kept referring to this future event as the Extraction. I felt like a reproduction of pregnancy in miniature. I no longer recognized my body. I was aware of the presence of something inside of me that in the end would not belong to me.

The day before *Roe v. Wade* was overturned. In another week, the eggs that are swelling inside me will be plucked then hatched by someone with good insurance who lives in the Upper East Side of Manhattan. The timing of these events feels too on the nose. The timing of the Extraction, my subsequent check for 10k, and when my MFA tuition is due is just about right.

The building used to depict "The Bramford" apartment building in the movie is located on the Upper West Side of Manhattan and is actually named the Dakota. Notably, it's also the site where John Lennon was murdered. A friend and I visited the Bramford/Dakota in the fall I moved to New York to chase poetry like it was a woman in a red raincoat. My friend and I both own flammable yellow nightgowns and have hair cropped above our ears. We both had been Rosemary on two separate Halloweens so we thought it something we both ought to see. There was no evidence of the witching going on inside. We could only see a well-dressed doorman sitting in a little glass box in front of the heavy, carved doors. All the windows lowest to the street had thick white curtains and a brass rod across the window. It was the middle of the day but there were glass lanterns flickering. Aside from the HOA fees there was nothing foreboding about it.

■ ■ ■

I know what the psychologist was trying to get me to understand when she kept asking me "But how would you *think* of the eggs?" during all my screening procedures before I was accepted to be in the donor program. There was a right answer and a wrong answer and I said the right one.

"I don't know? I don't know what they have to do with *me*."

When I first told my mother about the eggs and the impending Extraction, she said it was no different than leaving twenty-two babies at the fire station. I tried to explain supply and demand to my mother.

"People *want* those eggs. What am I going to use them for— breakfast?"

What the psychologist was trying to help me understand was that I had no control over these eggs once they hatched. Those eggs, under New York state law, could be used to make an antichrist, theoretically. I wondered what my moral role would be in the impending End of Days. As a child I had anxiety about the Rapture like other kids did about math class; I was nervous to be called upon.

■ ■ ■

I never understood why witches were scary. In *Rosemary's Baby*, they were just the hokey neighbors with bad taste in jewelry. Witches, like the devil, seemed as relevant a daily worry as a wasp. I wasn't particularly scared of wasps, but I knew where to watch out for them. My Mamaw worked at the first community health centers in Appalachia as a janitor in the nurses' dormitory. Eventually, she replaced the nurses who came down from the suburbs of Chicago and never lasted more than a season in Leslie County. Mamaw worked at the front desk of the clinic and saw some patients herself. She used to tell me all about the girls who came in bleeding and sick because they had visited the purple door women for help fixing "a little problem." *Granny witches*, another name. Witching and god lived in the mountains the same.

As a child, I was more afraid of god than I was of the devil. This might have been His design. I have worried about something being slipped inside my body without my notice. As a child, I grew up going to the churches that would sometimes meet in tents. During sermons, people were prone to swaying and calling out. At revivals, people collapsed on the ground, convulsed, or did cartwheels through the pews. I was terrified I was going to get struck next. Even the most innocuous of movements, like slipping up one hand, eyes bowed, and swaying, could put me in the notice of Something. I could get snatched up next.

Body as temple. Body as temple.

This was a home invasion threat more than an encouragement to go to the gym. My body is a house. I was afraid the real owner would come home and find all the lights had been left on.

■ ■ ■

The person I watched the movie with says that Rosemary and I are eerily similar.

"It's the haircut," I said, and told them, again, that I was Rosemary for Halloween. I describe the stuffed lamb I carried with me all night.

No. It's not that. It's because you also always do what you're told and always try to avoid inconveniencing people. And you only say stuff to stick up for yourself about half the time.

■ ■ ■

In New York, they say people don't know their neighbors. This is not true. I know precisely when my upstairs neighbor rises to get ready for work and I know when my downstairs neighbor gets home from work. They both work as people who stomp, probably using their bare feet to mush around grapes in wood tubs till they become wine. Towards the end of the movie, it's the soft sound of a baby crying next door that rouses Rosemary up to stumble upon the cache of witches.

My Mamaw used to say that when a new neighbor moved in you should split your flower bulbs in half to give to them. Halving your flowers will double your yield. We used to take walks through the woods and find a cloister of easter lilies in a grassy clearing. Mamaw said they only grew where a house once was. A few miles from here there might be another clutch of yellow if this once was a homestead of neighborly people.

I am halving my yield now, hoping that what I reap comes in double. I am not giving because I am sweet. I give to get something more in return. I want to sit in a warm stone room and talk about poetry with classmates. I also want to pay my rent. This is a bigger return than letting those eggs slip by unnoticed and uncapitalized through my underwear each month.

I know so much of my neighbors' lives without saying more than "good morning"/"good night" by the mailbox. I am about to give something to a stranger. A person who knows very little about me, aside from my genetic history, will get a broken-off bulb of my own patchwork. In a few years, if high rent hasn't pushed me out of this city, I could be taking a walk and pass by an egg that's now a child, holding hands with its parent. I might nod, my near neighbor, and move on, none of us the wiser to our kinship.

■ ■ ■

I have body horror about half the time. My stomach is a snowglobe and there is something bouncing gently like a screen saver on the inside. My thighs are mangled with bruises and dried pinpricks of blood. I am wearing shorts. The person I am watching *Rosemary's Baby* with hasn't noticed my legs.

The overturning of *Roe* brings to mind all the nosey neighbors who are conspiring to occupy the rooms of my house with their *purpose*. My body, the body of others, will be worked into the dwellings for their convictions. I have been mentally prepared for the day when my body is not my own.

The person I watched *Rosemary's Baby* with was not disturbed by the news. I pointed to my stomach and joked that I was already getting the rooms of my house ready. He says that I'll be safer up here in New York than I was down in Kentucky. He seems to think that because he is safe, everyone is. He must not believe in witches or the devil because they have never held hands and danced around him or stepped out from behind a purple door.

Of course! All the witches and the devil that walk about are held there in the mountains and in those sparse wide places. "Of course, I'm still worried," I said. "I have the haircut for it." ■

AFTER THE FIRE

Lightning shaved the firs from
the ridge, a bare rocky jawline we scale tonight. What
scrubs remains feather the granite we
splay against, two supernovas who cannot
resist the other's heat. Above, shuddering constellations hold
back hungry, darting space. I bleed through the
sweatshirt sleeve, a ruddy spattering of stars
all that separates us under emerald-splintered skies. Are
we all that remains in a forest newly made?

ERIN MATHESON RITCHIE

SARATOGA

Night yawns and swallows the Mustang whole as I step
into the backseat and close my eyes through
her unpracticed touch, my spine contouring a final lie as the back
windows shatter. My God, how anyone could fly straight
under a coal-charred moon, a final drive, her chin
tucked into mine. Twin precision engines built to flare up
and fizzle out, but we flip in a wreck that demands eyes,
witnesses, wagging tongues eager to pick our bones from the open
wreckage, peel our tights from trembling legs, staunch the heart
howling for another lap as her passenger, a future for us lively and loud.

ERIN MATHESON RITCHIE

CONTRIBUTORS

Daisy Bassen is a poet and community child psychiatrist who graduated from Princeton University's Creative Writing Program and completed her medical training at The University of Rochester and Brown. Her work has been published in *Salamander, McSweeney's, Smartish Pace, Crab Creek Review, Plume, Little Patuxent Review, New York Quarterly,* and *[PANK]* among other journals. She was the winner of the So to Speak 2019 Poetry Contest, the 2019 ILDS White Mice Contest, the 2020 Beullah Rose Poetry Prize, and the 2022 Erskine J Poetry Prize. She was nominated for the 2019, 2021, and 2022 *Best of the Net* Anthology and for a 2019, 2020, and 2022 Pushcart Prize. Born and raised in New York, she lives in Rhode Island with her family.

Mac Collins is an MFA in Creative Writing recipient from the University of Washington. Originally from Atlanta, Georgia, he now lives in Seattle where he works as a bartender and writing tutor when not occupied with poetry.

Carrie Conners, originally from West Virginia, lives in Queens, New York and is an English professor at LaGuardia Community College-CUNY. Her first poetry collection, *Luscious Struggle* (BrickHouse Books, 2019), was a 2020 Paterson Poetry Prize Finalist. Her second collection, *Species of Least Concern* was a finalist for the Main Street Rag Poetry Book Award (Main Street Rag, 2022). Her poetry has been nominated for a Pushcart Prize and has appeared in *Bodega, Kestrel, Split Rock Review, RHINO,* and *The Monarch Review,* among other publications. She is also the author of the book, *Laugh Lines: Humor, Genre, and Political Critique in Late Twentieth-Century American Poetry* (University Press of Mississippi, 2022).

Chelyen Davis's writing has previously appeared in publications such as *Appalachian Review, Still: The Journal, the Anthology of Appalachian Writers,* and *The Bitter Southerner.* A native of Southwest Virginia, she currently lives in Richmond, Virginia.

Makayla Danielle Gay hails from Southeastern Kentucky. Her work has appeared in *Adroit, American Literary Review, Appalachian*

Review, and *Prairie Schooner.* Her debut poetry collection, *Hackles,* is out now from Girl Noise Press.

Evan Gurney teaches English literature at the University of North Carolina, Asheville. His poems and essays have appeared recently or are forthcoming in *New Ohio Review, storySouth, Tar River Poetry, The Hopkins Review, Whale Road Review,* and elsewhere.

Luke Harvey lives with his wife and two daughters in Chickamauga, Georgia, at their small farm, Oak Haven. His work has appeared or is forthcoming in journals such as *Spiritus, The Christian Century, Delta Poetry Review, St. Katherine Review,* and elsewhere. His first collection, *Let's Call it Home,* is a member of the Poiema Poetry Series by Cascade Books. Harvey works primarily as a high school English teacher, but also runs the Oak Haven Writing Workshops.

Laura Johnsrude is a retired pediatrician living in Louisville, Kentucky. Her essays have been published or are forthcoming in *Fourth Genre, Bellevue Literary Review, River Teeth, Hippocampus, The Spectacle, Please See Me, Minerva Rising, Drunk Monkeys, Under the Gum Tree, The Examined Life Journal, Sweet: A Literary Confection, The Boom Projectanthology,* and on *Brevity*'s Nonfiction Blog. Johnsrude's piece, "Drawing Blood," won Honorable Mention for *Bellevue Literary Review*'s spring 2018 Fel Felice Buckvar Prize for Nonfiction. Her book reviews have been published in *Good River Review.*

Mikey Jones (he/they) is a queer Appalachian poet currently living in Seattle, Washington. He is the co-editor of *Grief Journeys,* an anthology of grief from The Healing Center. His poetry appears in *Screen Door Review, Hood of Bone Review,* and *Susurrus Magazine,* among other publications. Jones enjoys tending to their houseplants, long walks in the woods, and books that make him cry. Find more of their work at mikeybjones.com

Devon Neal (he/him) is a Bardstown, Kentucky resident who received a B.A. in Creative Writing from Eastern Kentucky University and an MBA from the University of the Cumberlands. He currently works as a Human Resources Manager in Louisville. His work has been featured in *Moss Puppy Magazine, Dead Peasant, Paddler Press, MIDLVLMAG,* and other publications.

Erin Matheson Ritchie lives in California with her spouse and pet rabbit. She earned her master's degree in education at Stanford University, taught secondary English for seven years, and caught a piranha while fishing at an Amazon River research facility. Her poems appear in *New Feathers Anthology, Cosmic Daffodil*, and *Dog Teeth*.

Austin Sanchez-Moran is a teacher and Pushcart Prize nominated writer who received his MFA in Poetry from George Mason University. His poems and short fiction have been published in *RHINO, Denver Quarterly, and Salamander Magazine,* among many other publications. He also has had poems and short fiction chosen for the anthologies, *Best New Poets of the Midwest* (2017) and *Best Microfiction 2020*, respectively. His first poetry collection is *Suburban Sutras* (Finishing Line Press, 2021) and his first chapbook, *Rhinocerotica* (Backbone Press, 2022), was selected by Tyree Daye as winner of the 4th Annual Backbone Press Chapbook Competition.

John Schneider is the author of, *Swallowing the Light* (2022), a Pinnacle Best Book Poetry winner, NYC Big Book Distinguished Favorite, International Book Awards winner, and Hoffer Award nominee, and *And Our Bodies Again Make Sense*, forthcoming in 2025. His nonfiction book, *Dreaming and Being Dreamt,* was published by Routledge in 2023. Schneider is a multiple award-winning poet, most recently winner of the Milton Kessler Prize for Poetry, and a finalist for the Steve Kowit Prize, as well as *The Atlanta Review* International Poetry Competition, the Rash Award and *Crosswinds* Poetry Contest. He resides in Berkeley, California.

George Singleton has published thirteen books, including *These People Are Us; The Half-Mammals of Dixie; Why Dogs Chase Cars; Novel; Drowning in Gruel; Work Shirts for Madmen; Pep Talks, Warnings, and Screeds; Stray Decorum; Between Wrecks; Calloustown; Staff Picks; You Want More: Selected Stories.* He has also published over two hundred stories in magazines and journals like the *Atlantic Monthly, Harper's One Story, Playboy, Georgia Review, Zoetrope, North American Review, Story, LitMag, Southern Review, Mid-American Review, Fiction International, The Quarterly, Carolina Quarterly, Agni, Oxford American, Virginia Quarterly Review, Five Points, Black Warrior Review, Subtropics, Texas Review*, and *Glimmer Train.* He lives in Spartanburg, South Carolina.

Heather Swain is the author of novels for adults and young adults (as H.A. Swain), illustrated children's books, personal essays and short stories. Her most recent short fiction, "Pool Robot," appeared in *Southern Humanities Review.* She grew up exploring the woods and playing in creeks in central Indiana. "Bullfrog" is based on an anaphylactic reaction she had while deep in the Pisgah National Forest near Blowing Rock, North Carolina. She now lives with her family in Brooklyn, New York where she teaches children to read when she's not in walking the trails in Prospect Park with her dog.

Heather Truett holds an MFA from the University of Memphis and is doing PhD work at FSU. Her debut novel, *Kiss and Repeat,* was released from Macmillan in 2021. She has work in *Hunger Mountain, Sweet Lit, Whale Road Review,* and other publications. Heather serves as editor-in-chief for the *Southeast Review.* Find out more at www. heathertruett.com.

www.ingramcontent.com/pod-product-compliance
Lightning Source LLC
Chambersburg PA
CBHW070605180626
46817CB00005B/1997